THE
CONVERSATION MANUAL

A COLLECTION OF 670 USEFUL PHRASES
IN
ENGLISH, HINDUSTANI, PERSIAN AND PASHTU

THE CONVERSATION MANUAL

A COLLECTION OF 670 USEFUL PHRASES
IN
ENGLISH, HINDUSTANI, PERSIAN AND PASHTU
WITH
SUMMARIES OF THE GRAMMARS OF THESE LANGUAGES,
AND
VOCABULARY OF NEARLY 1500 WORDS

CAPTAIN G. T. PLUNKETT

GYAN

Published by

GYAN

Gyan Publishing House
5, Ansari Road
Daryaganj, New Delhi-110002
Phone: 011-47034999, 9811692060
E-mail: books@gyanbooks.com

Distribution Network
gyanbooks.com
India, USA, Canada, UK, Australia, France

ISBN : 978-81-212-4279-0 (PB)
First Published, London, 1875

2nd Impression 2020

Printed at: Gyan Press, Delhi.

THE

CONVERSATION MANUAL,

A COLLECTION OF 670 USEFUL PHRASES

IN

ENGLISH, HINDUSTANI, PERSIAN AND PASHTŪ

WITH

SUMMARIES OF THE GRAMMARS OF THESE LANGUAGES,

AND A

VOCABULARY OF NEARLY 1500 WORDS,

For the use of Engineer Officers and others on the North-West Frontier and in India.

BY CAPTAIN G T. PLUNKETT

ROYAL ENGINEERS.

London:

RICHARDSON & CO., 23, CORNHILL, E.C.,
& 13, PALL MALL, S.W.

1875.

CONTENTS.

PART I.

	PAGE
The Alphabet	9
Elements of Hindūstānī Grammar	13
Elements of Persian Grammar	17
Elements of Pashtū Grammar	21

PART II.

SENTENCES—

Section I.	Nouns and Verbs	33
	Note—(These sentences comprise examples on the declensions and conjugations, and illustrate the Grammars.)	
... II.	General Orders and Questions	38
... III.	Orders to Cook and Table Servant	46
... IV.	Seasons and Weather	50
... V.	Numbers, Time and Age	52
... VI.	Money, Weights and Measures	55
... VII.	Books and Office Work	58
... VIII.	Travelling and Shooting	60
... IX.	Reconnoitring	67
... X.	Surveying	76
... XI.	Artificer's Work and Building	78
... XII.	Military Terms	88
... XIII.	Sickness and Remedies	91

PART III.

Vocabulary and Index to Sentences	95

CONTENTS

PREFACE.

So long as England retains her present position in Asia, and seems not unlikely to extend over other parts of the Continent the influence which she already exerts in the countries bordering on Hindūstān, it is very desirable that a knowledge of Persian —the French of Asia, and the most widely-spoken language from the Bosphorus to the confines of China, a tongue understood on the shores of the Caspian as well as in Kābul and Yārkand—should be more generally diffused among British Officers; and that this knowledge should embrace a practical acquaintance with the colloquial idioms, as well as proficiency in the text-books used for the Examinations.

Pashtū is the language of Eastern Afghānīstān, and, though useless elsewhere, is almost indispensable for those who are employed on the North-West Frontier of India.

On arriving for the first time in Peshāwar, and attempting to converse with Kābulees and others in Persian, I found myself frequently at a loss for the phrases required in ordinary conversation and for technical words; I also discovered how very advantageous even a slight knowledge of Pashtū must be to an officer serving in this district.

I therefore set to work, whenever I could spare time from professional duties, to write down a number of sentences in English, with their equivalents in Persian and Pashtū, somewhat after the model of the three or four Hindūstānī Manuals already in use, but in a more methodical manner and on a more comprehensive scale.

Believing that no such useful collection of phrases relating to the occurrences of everyday life, as well as to the special occupations of Engineers, is to be found elsewhere, I have added the Urdū, in the hope that this may render the Work of service to brother officers and others in India as well as on the Frontier, and have prefixed such brief abstracts of the Hindūstānī, Persian and Pashtū Grammars as will suffice for those who wish to obtain a colloquial knowledge only of any of these languages. The Vocabulary, which also forms an index to the sentences, gives the equivalents of nearly 1500 words in common use.

In compiling this little Work I have been aided by Saiyad Khādim Alī, a subordinate of the Military Works Department; and I have received great assistance from Ḳāzī Mahmūd Khān Khatak, the well-known teacher of languages in Peshāwar, more especially in the Pashtū, but also in the revision and correction of the whole.

I cannot expect that this Manual will be free from imperfections, either in the Pashtū—a language in which almost as many dialects are met with as there are tribes among the Afghāns, and of which the spelling has not yet been reduced to a regular system—or even in the Persian; but can only hope that these may not be so numerous as to detract from its value to those for whom it is intended, and that I may be allowed to plead as an excuse for deficiencies or inaccuracies the very few leisure hours which I have been able to devote to this Work.

G. T. P.

Peshāwar, February, 1875.

LIST OF ERRATA.

The Alphabet: p. 9, 5th line from the bottom, *ṅ* should be *ṅṛ*.
p. 10, u . . . . *u* in rule, should be ū . . . . *u in rule.*

Hindustani Grammar: p. 13, Pronouns, Genitive Case, for *mer-i*, read *mer-ī.*
p. 15, 9th line from the bottom, for *dīūṅ*, read *deūṅ*.

Pashtū Grammar: p. 21, omit "4. Nouns in *ah*," &c. (N.B. The mute *h* having been omitted in this work, these Nouns are included under Class 1, Nouns in *a*.)
p. 21. Declension of Nouns, in Genitive Case and Ablative, for *saṛi*, read *saṛī*.
p. 22. Personal Pronouns, 5th line from bottom, for "In." (Instrumental Case), read "Agent."
p. 23, line 4, after { Masc. *hag͟huh* / Fem. *hag͟he* } read Plur. *hag͟ho*.
" last line but one, for *Tāso yae*, read *Tāso yaī*.
" last line, for *Hag͟hoè dè*, read *Hag͟hoī dī*.

IN THE HINDUSTANI, Part II.

Sect.	No.				
I.	2	*for*	betā	*read*	beṭā.
	9	"	tumhare	"	tumhāre.
	39	"	k͟hargash	"	k͟hargosh.
VI.	27	"	ḥissāb	"	ḥisāb.
VII.	12	"	ṣafḥa	"	ṣafḥe.
VIII.	27	"	sīr	"	sir.
	41	"	alag	"	alag alag.
	44	"	gāṛhī	"	gāṛī.
	49	"	ek na'l ghoṛe	"	ek ghoṛe.
	53	"	laje	"	lage.
	57	"	ikhatte	"	ikatthe.
IX.	30	"	loge	"	lage.
	41	"	k͟haṛe	"	khaṛe.
X.	1	"	apnā	"	apnī
XI.	3	"	purī	"	pūrī.
	69	"	khoā	"	roṛa.
	74	"	dube	"	ḍūbe.
XII.	6	"	gārḍ meṅ	"	gārat par.
	17	"	dhu rā	"	dhurā.
	30	"	he	"	ke.

LIST OF ERRATA.

In Part III., the following are correct, in place of the words as printed:—

Cart	gāṛī	Hollow	k͟halī	Procrastination	ṭāl māṭolī.
Danger	dahshat	Horn	sing	Rudder	patwār.
Garlic	thūm	Laugh, to	hansnā	Soup	shorwa.
Green	harā	Pouch	toshdān	Splash, to	chhiṛknā.
Hip	chutaṛ	Prison	jelk͟hāna	Stack, to	k͟haṛwanjā l.

IN THE PERSIAN, Part II.

Sect. I.	2	*for*	ṭifl	*read*	ṭifl.
	14	„	an	„	ān.
	23	„	bala	„	bālā.
II.	13	„	bāwarchī	„	āshpaz.
	13	„	bitalab	„	biṭalab.
	24	„	binishin	„	binishīn.
III.	2	„	mez tok	„	nān biyār.
	36	„	biyawezānd	„	biyāwézān.
V.	13 & 14	„	chaud	„	chand (also omit ha before hastand).
VI.	27	„	ḥissāb	„	ḥisāb.
VII.	5	„	saḥīh	„	saḥīḥ.

The following readings should be substituted in Part III.:—

Agree, to	kabūl k.	Damage	nuḳṣān	Irrigation	ābpāshī.
Almanac	taḳwīm	Diagonal	munḥanī	Ivory	dandān i fīl.
Beam	tīr	Divorce	ṭalāk	Land	zamīn.
Box	ṣandūḳ	Fig	anjīr	Lend, to	ḳarẓ dādan.
Brother	birādar	Fine	jarīmāna	Litter	k͟has o k͟hāshāk.
Cheque	kāg͟haẕ i zar	Gallop, to	dawānīdan	Niche	ṭāḳ.
Chess	shaṭranj	Gram	nak͟hud	Reservoir	ḥauẓ.
Cocoanut	nārjīl	Halting-place	manzil	Rot, to	ganda shudan.
Come, to	āmadan			Rudder	suk͟hān.
Cook	āshpaz	Hire	kirāya	Sheet	chādar.
Cream	ḳaimāg͟h	Hollow	kāwāk	Shirt	ḳamīṣ, &c.
Creditor	ḳarẓk͟hwāh	Influence	zarī'a	Span	bidast.

Thick, g͟haliẓ, &c.

IN THE PASHTŪ, Part II.

Sect. I.	10	*for*	zoi	*read*	dzoe.
	25	„	dzāi	„	dzāe.
	25	„	razai	„	rādzaī.
	55	„	hag͟hoe	„	hag͟ho.
	62	„	hag͟ha	„	hag͟hub.
	62	„	līdalaī	„	līdalai.
	64	„	tālī	„	talī.
	65	„	wah	„	wai.

LIST OF ERRATA.

SECT. I.	65	*for*	zalī dī	*read*	dzalede.
	67	„	bahī dī	„	bahede.
	73	„	pa . . . pa	„	da . . . da.
II.	62	„	rāgarze	„	rāgarzedalai.
	70	„	tol i	„	ṭole.
	102	„	plana	„	ūgda.
	109	„	her no ke	„	maherawa.
III.	12	„	shande	„	shaude.
	30	„	shue	„	shne.
	35	„	ghwa pai	„	ghwā paī.
	37	„	wabāsa	„	wubāsa.
	41	„	tā tsa	„	tuh tsuh.
IV.	11	„	waredatī	„	waredalī.
	12	„	shū	„	shuh.
	21	„	wuh	„	wah.
V.	6	„	atallaso	„	da atallaso.
	10	„	shīwī	„	shawī.
	14	„	g͟hāwe	„	ghwāwe.
VI.	1	„	ra	„	pa.
VIII.	16	„	k͟hima	„	k͟heme.
	24	„	pse	„	warbānde.
	30	„	pareye	„	pore ye.
	76	„	pa toke	„	pa pato ke.
IX.	78	„	zuh	„	dza.
	81	„	zāngana	„	zangānuh.
X.	6	„	ye ma	„	ye.
	9	„	hi	„	chi.
XI.	15	„	k͟hkarākegī	„	k͟hkārakegī.
XII.	24	„	ghobal	„	zhobal.
XIII.	9	„	nare	„	nore.

In the Pashtū, Part III., substitute the following :—

Absent	g͟hāib	Extinguish, to	mṛawal	Police station	tsaukaī.
Adze	tarkk͟hadz	Field	paṭai	Printer	chāpka-wūnkai.
Bath	g͟husl	Flurry, to	ḍarawal	Quince	bihaī.
Bite, to	chīchal	Fox	lumbaṛa	Ripe	pok͟h.
Bone	haḍūkai	Green	shīn	Round, to go	garzedal.
Brave	zaṛawar	Hat	ṭopaī	Sailor	māṅṛgai.
Cautery	dāg͟h	Hollow	tash	Sedan	pālkaī.
Cart	gāḍai	Home, at	pa kor ke	Sleeve	lastūṅṛai.
Cross out, to	ḳalam rāk͟hal	Hot	garm	Spin, to	owdal.
Dead	maṛai, maṛ	Immediately	sam da lāsa	Till	tar-pore.
Dear	'azīz	Ink	sıyāhī	Top hill	tsūka.
Doorbar	aṛamai	Light, to	balawal	Umbrella	chatraī.
Double	dwadzala	Lucerne	shautala	Weave, to	owdal.
Drum	ḍol	Newspaper	ak͟hbār	Weaver	julāha.
End	āk͟hir	Pear	nāspātaī		
Equal	barābar				

Why, wale, tsuh la.

PART I.

THE ALPHABET.

THE POWERS OF THE VARIOUS LETTERS USED.

The Consonants.

Additional letters in Hindi.	The Persian Alphabet.	Additional letters in Pashtū.	PRONUNCIATION.
	b		as *b*.
	p		as *p*.
	t		the soft *t*, as in the Italian language.
ṭ		ṭ	as *t* in *rat*.
	s̤		as *s* in *sin*.
	j		as *j*.
		dz	as *z*.
	ch		as *ch* in *chin*.
		ts	as *ts* or *s*.
	ḥ		as *h*, but strongly aspirated.
	kh		as the German *ch* in *buch*.
	d		the soft *d*, as in the Italian language.
ḍ		ḍ	as *d*.
	ẕ		as *z*.
	r		as *r*.
ṛ		ṛ	a stronger *r*, pronounced with the tip of the tongue turned up.
	z		as *z* in *zeal*.
	zh		as *z* in *azure*.
		ġ	as *g*.
	s		as *s*.

Additional letters in Hindi.	The Persian Alphabet.	Additional letters in Pashtū.	PRONUNCIATION.
	sh		as *sh*.
		kkh	as *kh*.
	ṣ		as *ṣ*.
	ẓ		as *z*.
	ṭ		as *t*.
	ẓ		as *z*.
	'		(the Arabic ' ain), a guttural sound unknown in English.
	gh		a guttural sound, something like *g*.
	f		as *f*.
	ḳ		a guttural *k*, like the *c* in *acquire*.
	k		as *k*.
	g		as *g* in *gun*.
	l		as *l*.
	m		as *m*.
	n		as *n*: when written *ṅ* it is nasal, as in *anchor*.
		ṅ	a nasal sound of *ṅ* and *ṛ* combined.
	w		as *w*.
	h		as *h*.
	y		as *y*.

The foregoing table is according to the most approved method of representing the various Consonants of the Oriental Alphabets by English letters and symbols; thus the *t* and the *ṭ* represent respectively the soft *t* common to the Hindī and the Persian Alphabets, and the hard *ṭ* which is peculiar to the Hindī and Pashtū. The *h* represents the soft aspirate common to all, and the *ḥ* the strong aspirate of certain Arabic words. The object of making these distinctions in this Work is to enable anyone to write out the phrases correctly in the Oriental characters; but the learner who only wishes to acquire a colloquial knowledge may treat the *t*, *ṭ*, and *ṭ̤* as *t*, the *s*, *ṣ*, and *s̤* as *s*, and so on: he should, however, learn the true sound of the *g͟h* (g͟hain) from the natives.

It must be noted that *ph*, *th*, *dh*, &c., are to be pronounced as the *ph* in *up-hill*, the *th* in *hot-house*, the *dh* in *mad-house*, &c.; *ẉ* with a dot underneath is not to be sounded; a final short *a* represents the final *ah* of many Persian words in which the *h* is silent.

The vowel sounds are—

a, pronounced as *u* in *fun*, or *a* in *America*.
i, ... *i* in *fin*.
u, ... *u* in *push*.
ā, ... *a* in *father*.
ī, ... *i* in *police*.
ū, ... *u* in *rule*.
o, ... *o* in *pole*.
au, ... *ou* in *sound*.
e, ... *a* in *grave*.
ai, ... *ai* in *aisle*.

In Hindūstānī and in Persian the sounds of the Consonants and Vowels never vary. And this is generally the rule in Pashtū, but with some exceptions; for instance, it is difficult to decide whether the Pashtū for "water" should be written *obuh* or *oba*, the sound in the last syllable being nearly that of the German *ö* in schönen.

The above tables give as nearly as possible the pronunciation of the Hindūstānīs of the North-west Provinces, the Afg͟hāns of the Yūsufzai tribe, and the Persians of the Kābul and Herāt. The western tribes of Afg͟hānstān pronounce the *k͟kh* as *ksh*, and the *ġ* as *zh;* while the *ts* varies in sound between *s* and *z*. It is sufficient, however, to learn the eastern dialect of Yūsufzāi, which is everywhere intelligible.

The inhabitants of Persia soften the *ā* in many words into *ū;* thus, *ān*, "that," is pronounced *ūn*, and *kaliyān*, "a pipe," *kaliyūn;* and they sound the short *a* like the English short *a* in "fan," instead of that in "fun;" thus, *bale*, "yes," is pronounced by them like our word *ballet*, but with a drawl, which lengthens the first syllable. They also soften *e* into *ī;* for instance, *mī rawed*, "you go," is pronounced *mī rawīd*.

ELEMENTS OF HINDUSTANI GRAMMAR.

There is no Article: to express *the* in the Accusative Case, the Dative with *ko* is used. (*See Phrases, Nos.* 38 *and* 39, *Section I. of Part II.*). *ī* is generally the feminine termination of Nouns and Adjectives. Nouns ending in *t* and *sh* are also mostly feminine.

The Noun is declined thus :—

Sing.	*Plur.*
Nom., *mard*, man	*mard*, men
Gen., *mard-kā -ke -kī*, of man	*mardoṅ-kā -ke -kī*, of men
Dat., *mard-ko*, to man	*mardoṅ-ko*, to men [men
Acc., *mard-ko* or *mard*, the man	*mardoṅ-ko* or *mard*, the men or
Abl., *mard se*, &c., from man	*mardoṅ se*, &c., from the men, or
Agent, *mard ne*, man (used only with past tenses of transitive verbs).	*mardoṅ ne*, men [men

In fem. nouns, to the nom. plural is added *eṅ* or *yāṅ*; thus, *mez*, 'a table,' *mezeṅ*, *mezoṅ kā*, &c.; *roṭī*, 'bread,' *roṭiyān*, *roṭiyoṅ ka*, &c. Nouns ending in *ā* and *a*, generally change these into *e* in the oblique cases and plural; thus, *kuttā*, 'a dog;' *kutte kā*, 'of a dog;' *kutte*, 'dogs;' *kuttoṅ kā*, &c. Adjectives in *ā* similarly take *ī* in the fem., as *achchhā mard*, 'a good man;' *achchhī laṛkī*, 'a good girl;' and *e* in the oblique cases and plural, as *achchhe mard kā laṛkā*, 'a good man's son.'

THE PRONOUNS.

Singular.	*Plural.*
Nom., *maiṅ*, I	*ham*, we
Gen., *merā -e -i*, my [me	*hamārā -e -ī*, our
Dat. and Acc., *mujh ko*, to me or	*ham ko*, to us, *or* us
Abl., *mujh se*, from me	*ham se*, from us
Agent, *maiṅ ne*, I	*ham ne*, we

Singular.	*Plural.*
Nom., *tū*, thou	*tum*, you
Gen., *terā -e -ī*, thy [thee	*tumhārā -e -ī*, your
Dat. and Acc., *tujh ko*, to thee, *or*	*tum ko*, to you, *or* you
Abl., *tujh se*, from thee	*tum se*, by you
Agent, *tū ne*, thou	*tum ne*, you.

YIH, 'this,' 'he,' 'she,' or 'it.'

Singular.	*Plural.*
Nom. *yih*, Gen. *is kā*, Dat. *is ko*, &c.	*ye*, *in kā*, &c.

WUH, 'that,' 'he,' 'she,' or 'it.'

Singular.	*Plural.*
Nom. *wuh*, Gen. *uskā*, Dat. *usko*, &c.	*we*, *unkā*, &c.
Interrog. who? *kaun*, Gen. *kiskā*, &c.	*kaun kin kā*, &c.
Relative, who, *jo jiskā*, &c.	*jo jinkā*, &c.
Correl. that same, *so*, *tiskā*, &c.	*so*, *tiṅ kā*, &c.
Interrog. what? *kyā*, *kāhe kā*, &c.	

Āp, 'self,' or 'your honour.' *Apnā -e -i*, 'own;' *koī*, 'any;' *kuchh*, 'some.'

AUXILIARY VERB.

Present, Sing. *maiṅ hūṅ*, I am; *tū hai*, *wuh hai*.
Plur. *ham haiṅ*, We are; *tum ho*, *we haiṅ*.
Past, Sing. *maiṅ thā* (fem. *thī*), I was, *tū thā*, *wuh thā*.
Plur. *ham the* fem. *thīṅ*), We were, *tum the*, *we the*.

REGULAR NEUTER VERB.

Girnā, to fall; *girt-ā* (fem. *-ī*, pl. *-e* and *-īṅ*), falling; *gir-ā* (fem. *-ī*, pl. *-e* and *īṅ*), fallen—root, *gir*.

AORIST.

Sing. *maiṅ girūṅ*, I may fall, *tū gire*, *wuh gire*.
Plur. *ham gireṅ*, We may fall, *tum giro*, *we gireṅ*.

FUTURE.

Maiṅ girūng-ā, *-ī*, I shall fall, *tū gireg-ā*, *-ī*, &c.

IMPERATIVE.

Sing. *gir*, fall.	Plur. *giro*, fall ye.

THE INDEFINITE.—I fall, &c.

Sing. *maiṅ girt-ā* (fem. *ī*), &c.	Plur. *ham girt-e* (fem. *īṅ*), &c.

THE PRESENT.—I am falling.

Sing. *maiṅ girt-ā hūṅ*, &c.	Plur. *ham girt-e haiṅ*, &c.

THE IMPERFECT.—I was falling.

Sing. *maiṅ girt-ā thā* (fem. *girt-ī thī*), &c.
Plur. *ham girt-e the* (fem. *girt-ī thīn*), &c.

PAST.—I fell.

Sing. *maiṅ gir-ā* (fem. *-ī*), &c.	Plur. *ham gir-e* (*īn*), &c.

PERFECT.—I have fallen.

Sing. *maiṅ girā hūṅ* (fem. *girī hūn*), &c.
Plur. *ham gire haiṅ* (fem. *girī haiṅ*), &c.

PLUPERFECT.—I had fallen.

Sing. *maiṅ girā thā* (fem. *girī thī*), &c.
Plur. *ham gire the* (fem. *girī thīn*), &c.

Transitive Verbs take the Agent Case, with the Past, Perfect and Pluperfect Tenses; thus, *khānā*, 'to eat;' Aorist, *maiṅ khāūṅ*. Present, *maiṅ khātā hūṅ*, &c.; Past, *maiṅ ne khāyā*, *tū ne khāyā*, &c.; Perfect, *maiṅ ne khāyā hai*, *tū ne khāyā hai*, &c.; Pluperfect, *maiṅ ne khāyā thā*, *tū ne khāyā thā*, &c.

The Passive Voice is formed by using the past participle with the verb *jānā*, 'to go' (*jātā*, 'going,' *gayā*, 'gone'); thus, *maiṅ khāyā jāūṅ* (fem. *khāī jāūṅ*), 'I may be eaten;' *ham khāe jāenge* (fem. *khāī jāeṅgīn*), we shall be eaten.' Past, *maiṅ khāyā gayā*, 'I was eaten,' &c.

There are no Irregular Verbs in Hindūstānī; but in some cases the Regular Past Participle has become obsolete, and the Past Participle of another Verb, of similar meaning, and of which the Present Tense has fallen into disuse, is used in its place; thus, *jānā*, 'to go;' *jātā*, 'going;' *gayā*, 'gone.' Some contractions are also made for the sake of euphony, as from *denā*, 'to give,' *dūṅ*, 'I may give,' is generally used instead of *diūṅ*, Past Participle *diyā*, 'given.'

The days of the week are named thus:—

Sunday,	*itwār.*
Monday,	*somwār*, or *pīr.*
Tuesday,	*mangalwār.*
Wednesday,	*budh.*
Thursday,	*juma' rāt.*
Friday,	*juma'.*
Saturday,	*sanīchar.*

THE CARDINAL NUMBERS IN HINDUSTANI.

1	ek	26	chhabbīs	51	ikāwan	76	chhihattar
2	do	27	satā, is	52	bāwan	77	sathattar
3	tīn	28	aṭhā, īs	53	tirpan	78	aṭhhattar
4	chār	29	untīs	54	chauwan	79	unāsi
5	pānch	30	tīs	55	pachpan	80	assi
6	chha	31	iktīs	56	chhappan	81	ikāsī
7	sāt	32	batīs	57	sattāwan	82	be, asī.
8	āṭh	33	taiṅtīs	58	aṭhāwan	83	tirāsī
9	nau	34	chauṇtīs	59	unsaṭh	84	chaurāsī
10	das	35	paiṅtīs	60	sāṭh	85	pachāsī
11	gyārah	36	chhattīs	61	iksaṭh	86	chhi, āsī
12	bārah	37	saiṅtīs	62	bāsaṭh	87	satāsī
13	terah	38	aṭhtīs	63	tirsaṭh	88	aṭhāsī
14	chaudah	39	untālīs	64	chausaṭh	89	nau, āsī
15	pandrah	40	chālīs	65	paiṅsath	90	nauwe
16	solah	41	iktālīs	66	chhi, āsath	91	ikānawe
17	satrah	42	be, ālīs	67	satsaṭh	92	bānawe
18	aṭhārah	43	taiṅtālīs	68	aṭhsaṭh	93	tirānawe
19	unīs	44	chau,ālīs	69	unhattar	94	chaurānawe
20	bīs	45	paiṅtālīs	70	sattar	95	pachānawe
21	ikkīs	46	chhi,ālīs	71	ikhattar	96	chhi, ānawe
22	bā, īs	47	saiṅtālīs	72	bahattar	97	satānawe
23	te, īs	48	aṛtālīs	73	tihattar	98	aṭhānawe
24	chaubīs	49	unchās	74	chauhattar	99	ninānawe
25	pachīs	50	pachās	75	pachhattar	100	sau or sai.

The Ordinal Numbers are—*pahlā*, 'first;' *dūsrā*, 'second;' *tīsrā*, 'third;' *chauthā*, 'fourth;' *panchwān*, 'fifth;' *chhatwān*, 'sixth;' *sātwān*, 'seventh;' and so on, regularly, for the remaining numbers, by adding *wān* to the Cardinals. They are declined like Adjectives; thus, *pahlā* and *pānchwān* become, in the oblique cases and plural, *pahle* and *pānchwen*, and in the feminine *pahlī* and *pānchwīn*. For the application of the Grammar, for instance, to learn when to use the genitive termination *-ke* instead of *-kā*, or to put the Adjective in the oblique case, the learner is referred to the phrases in Part II., Section I., which may with advantage be written as exercises.

ELEMENTS OF PERSIAN GRAMMAR.

There is no Article; but to express *the* in the Accusative Case the Dative (with *rā*) is used. (*See Phrases* 38, 39, *Section I.*) The genitive is formed by adding *i* (after a vowel *e*) to the governing noun; thus, *kitāb i man*, 'the book of me,' *or* 'my book.' The plural ends in *ān* for animate, *hā* for inanimate objects; thus, *mard*, *mardān*; *kitāb*, *kitabhā*: or after *a* thus, *banda*, 'a slave,' *bandagān*; *sūba*, 'a district,' *sūbajāt*, &c.

PRONOUNS.

Sing. *man*, I; *marā*, to me; *man* or *marā*, me. Plur. *mā*, we, &c.
Sing. *tū*, thou; *shumā*, you; *o*, he, she, or it. Plur. *eshān*, they.
Ki, who *or* which; *ki*, who? *chi*, which? *or* what? *kudām*, which? what sort of? *or* any?

VERBS.

Sing. *hastam*, I am; *hastī*, thou art; *hast*, he is.
Plur. *hastem*, *hasted*, *hastand*.
Also without the aspirate, *astam*, *astī*, *ast*, *astem*, *asted*, *astand*.
Also the simple affix, *am*, *ī*, *ast*, *em*, *ed*, *and*.
Sing., *būdam*, I was; *būdī*, thou wast; *būd*, he was.
Plur., *būdem*, *būded*, *būdand*.

Rasīdan, 'to arrive' (root, *ras*).
Rasān, 'arriving;' *rasīda*, 'arrived;' *rasanda*, 'an arriver.'

Tenses from the Root.

1st, *Aorist.*

Rasam, 'I may arrive;' *rasī*, 'thou mayest arrive;' *rasad*, the may arrive.'
Rasem, 'we may arrive; *rased*, 'you may arrive;' *rasand*, they may arrive.'

2nd, *Present.*—'I am arriving,' &c.

Sing., *Mīrasam*, *mīrasī*, *mīrasad*.
Plur., *mīrasem*, *mīrased*, *mīrasand*.

3rd, *Imperative.*—*Ras*, 'arrive thou;' plur., *rased*.

B

Tenses from the Infinitive.

1st, *The Past.*

Rasīdam, 'I arrived;' *rasīdī, rasīd.*
Plur. *rasīdem, rasīded, rasīdand.*

2nd, *Imperfect.*

Mī rasīdam, 'I was arriving;' *mīrasīdī, mīrasīd.*
Plur. *mīrasīdem, mīrasīded, mīrasīdand.*

3rd, *Past Potential.*—'I might arrive,' &c. (Seldom used. *See Section I., Phrases* 61 to 65).

Rasīdame, rasīdī, rasīde; rasīdeme, rasīdede, rasīdande.

4th, *Future.*

Khwāham rasīd, 'I shall arrive;' *khwāhī r., khhwāhad r.*
Plur. *khwāhem rasīd, khwāhed r., khwhāhand r.*

Tenses from Past Participle.

1st, *Perfect.*—'I have arrived.'

Rasīda am, rasīda ī, rasīda ast; plur., *rasīda em, rasīda ed, rasīda and.*

2nd, *Pluperfect.*—'I had arrived.'

Rasīda būdam,...būdī, ... būd; plur., *rasīda būdem, ... būded, ... būdand.*

The Roots are formed as follows:—

1. Infinitives in *adan, īdan* and *ādan* reject the termination: thus, *firistādan*, to send, *firist*; *pursīdan*, to ask, *purs*: except, *dādan*, to give, *dih*; *chīdan*, to collect, *chīn*; *dīdan*, to see, *bīn*; *āmadan*, to come, *ā* or *āy*; *zadan*, to strike, *zan*; *sitādan*, to seize, *sitān*; *āmādan*, to prepare, *āmā*; *zādan*, to bring forth, *zā*; *gādan*, to embrace, *gā*; *kushādan*, to open, *kushā*; *āfrīdan*, to create, *āfrīn*; *shunīdan*, to hear, *shunau*; *guzīdan*, to choose, *guzīn*.

2. Infinitives in *ūdan*, change it for *ā* or *āe*, as *sitūdan*, to praise, *sītāe* or *sitā*: except, *būdan*, to be, *bū* or *bash*; *shudan*, to be, *shaw*; *tanūdan*, to draw, *tanau*; *durūdan*, to reap, *durū*; *zinūdan*, to mingle, *zinau*; *ghunūdan*, to sleep, *ghunū*.

3. Infinitives in *rdan* or *udan* reject the *dan*, as *kandan*, to dig, *kan*: except, *āwurdan*, to bring, *ār* or *āwar*; *burdan*, to bear, *bar*; *kardan*, to do, *kun*; *murdan*, to die, *mīr*; *āzurdan*, to vex, *āzār*; *afshurdan*, to press, *afshār*; *sipurdan*, to entrust, *sipār*; *shumurdan*, to count, *shumār*; *farkandan*, to dig, *farkand*; *gandan*, to rot, *gand*.

4. Infinitives in *khtan* take *z*, as *andākhtan*, to throw, *andāz*: except, *shinākhtan*, to recognize, *shinās*; *farokhtan*, to sell, *farosh*;

gusikhtan, to break, *gusil*; *ākhtan*, to draw (a sword), *ākh*; *dokhtan*, to milk, *dosh*; *sukhtan*, to weigh, *sanj*.

5. Infinitives in *stan* reject the *stan*, as *zīstan*, to live, *zī*: except, *bastan*, to bind, *band*; *justan*, to seek, *jū*; *khāstan*, to rise, *khez*; *khwāstan*, to wish, *khwāh*; *paiwastan*, to join, *paiwand*; *justan*, to leap, *jah*; *rastan*, to escape, *rah*; *rustan*, to grow, *rūy*; *ristan*, to spin, *rīs*; *shustan*, to wash, *shūy*; *shikastan*, to break, *shikan*; *kāstan*, to diminish, *kāh*; *gusastan*, to break, *gusil*; *nishāstan*, to make to sit, *nishān*; *nishistan*, to sit, *nishīn*.

6. Infinitives in *shtan* take *r*, as *dāshtan*, to have, *dār*: except, *gashtan*, to become, *gard*; *nawishtan*, to write, *nawīs*; *hishtan*, to quit, *hil*; *āghāshtan*, to accumulate, *āghāsh*; *āghoshtan*, to embrace, *āghosh*; *afrāshtan*, to exalt, *afrāz*; *rishtan*, to spin, *rīs*; *kishtan*, to sow, *kār*; *kushtan*, to kill, *kush*.

7. Infinitives in *ftan* take *b*, as *tāftan*, to shine, *tāb*; or retain *f*, as *bāftan*, to weave, *bāf*: except, *khuftan*, to sleep, *khusp*; *raftan*, to go, *rau*; *giriftan*, to take, *gīr*; *guftan*, to say, *go* or *goy*; *pazīraftan* to accept, *pazīr*; *suftan*, to bore, *suft*; *shuguftan*, to blossom, *shuguft*; *shinuftan*, to hear, *shinau*; *kāftan*, to dig, *kāw*. Some are formed by lengthening the penult, as *ruftan*, to sweep, *rob*.

The days of the week are named thus in Persian :—

Sunday,	*yak shanba* (pronounced *shamba*).
Monday,	*do shanba*.
Tuesday,	*sih shanba*.
Wednesday,	*chahār shanba*.
Thursday,	*panj shanba*.
Friday,	*juma'*.
Saturday,	*shanba*.

CARDINAL NUMBERS IN PERSIAN AND PASHTŪ.

	Persian.	Pashtū.		Persian.	Pashtū
1	yak	yau	17	hafda	awah las
2	do	dwah	18	hezhda	atah las
3	sih	dre	19	nūzda	nah las
4	chahār	tsalor	20	bīst	shil
5	panj	pindzah	21	bīst o yak	yo wīsht
6	shash	shpag	30	sī	dersh
7	haft	awah	40	chihal	tsal wekkht
8	hasht	aṭah	50	panjāh	pindzos
9	nuh	nah	60	shaṣt	shpetah
10	dah	las	70	haftād	awiyah
11	yāzda	yo las	80	hashtād	atiyāh
12	duwāzda	dwa las	90	nuwad	nawe
13	sez-da	dyār las	100	ṣad	sil *or* sal
14	chahārda	tṣwār las	101	ṣad o yak	yau sil
15	pānzda	pindzahlas	1,000	hazār	zar
16	shānzda	shpāṛas	100,000	lak	lak

The ordinal numbers in Persian are formed thus:—

1st, *nukhustīn* or *awwal;* 2nd, *dūum* or *dūyum;* 3rd, *sūum* or *siyum;* 4th, *chahārum,* &c.

In Pashtū they are—1st, *awwal* or *wṛunbai;* 2nd, *dwayam*; 3rd, *dreyam;* 4th, *tsaloram,* &c.

ELEMENTS OF PASHTŪ GRAMMAR.

The Article is wanting, as in Urdū and Persian.

All Nouns are masculine or feminine. The following are usually feminine :—

1. Nouns in *a*, as *fāida*, advantage.
2. Nouns in *aī*, as *ṭopaī*, a hat.
3. Nouns in *ī*, as *badī*, evil.
4. Nouns in *ah*, as *zhibah*, tongue or language.
5. Purely Pashtū Nouns in *ā*, as *jāṛā*, crying.

The feminines are generally formed as follows :—

1. Masc. in *ai*, fem. in *aī* ; as, *spai*, a dog ; *spaī*, a bitch.
2. Masc. in *ī*, fem. in *aṅṛa* ; as, *dobī*, a washerman, *dobaṅṛa*.
3. Masc. in a consonant (except *ah*) add for fem. *a* ; as, *ūkh*, a camel, *ūkha*.
4. Masc. having *ū* in last syllable and masc. in *ah*, fem. in *ana* ; as, *shpūn*, a shepherd, *shpana* ; *ghobah*, a cowherd, *ghobana*.

Declension of Nouns.

1*st Declension*—Masculine Nouns in *ai* :—

	Singular.	*Plural.*
Nom.	*saṛai*, a man	*saṛī*.
Gen.	*da saṛi*, of a man	*da saṛiyo*.
Dat.	*saṛī ta*, to a man	*saṛiyo ta*.
Acc.	*saṛai*, a man	*saṛī*.
Abl.	*la saṛi na*, from a man	*la saṛiyo na*.
Locative.	*pa saṛī* (*kkhe*) *ke*, in a man	*pa saṛiyo* (*kkhe*) *ke*.
	pa saṛī bānde, upon a man	*pa saṛiyo bānde*.
	tar saṛī pore, up to a man	*tar saṛiyo pore*.
Agent	*saṛī*, by a man	*saṛiyo*.
Voc.	*ai Saṛiya*, Oh, man!	*ai saṛiyo*.

2*nd Declension*—Masculine Nouns ending in a consonant, and denoting inanimate objects :—Nom. *kor*, a house ; plur. *korūna*. Gen. *da kor*, of a house ; plur. *da korūno*. &c.

3rd Declension, Masculine—Nouns in a consonant, or *ī*, denoting animate objects; as, *mār*, a snake, *da mār;* plur. *mārān*, *da mārāno*, &c.

N.B. Many such Nouns are declined like the 2nd declension; as, *ās*, a horse, *āsūna*, &c.

4th Declension, Masculine—Nouns ending in a consonant denoting sounds; as, *krap*, a crunch, *da krap;* plur. *krapahār*, *da-krapahāro*, &c.

1st Declension, Feminine—Nouns in *aī* or *ī;* as, *spaī*, a bitch, *da spaī;* plur. *spaī*, *da spo*, &c.

2nd Declension, Feminine—Nouns in *a;* as, *khaza*, a woman, *da khaze;* plur. *khaze*, *da khazo*, &c.

3rd Declension, Feminine—Nouns in *ā;* as, *ghlā*, theft, *da ghlā;* plur. *ghle*, *da ghlāo*, &c.

4th Declension, Feminine—Nouns ending in consonants—*lār*, a road, *da lāre;* plur. *lāre*, *da lāro*, &c.

Adjectives are declined like Nouns, and agree in gender, number, and case.

The following form their feminines irregularly:—

Masc.	*tod*,	fem.	*tauda*,	hot.	Masc. *shīn*,	fem.	*shna*,	green.
...	*drund*,	...	*drana*,	heavy.	... *tor*,	...	*tora*,	black.
...	*trikh*,	...	*tarkha*,	bitter.	... *khog*,	...	*khwaga*,	sweet.
...	*trīw*,	...	*tarwā*,	sour.	... *khor*,	...	*khwara*,	scattered

Degrees of Comparison.

(*See Section I., Phrases* 11 *to* 14).

Personal Pronouns.

Nom.	*zuh*,	I,	Plur. *mūng*, we.	*tuh*,	thou,	Plur. *tāso*, you.
Gen.	*dzamā* or *da mā*	of me,	... *dzamūnga*.	*stā* or *datā*,	of thee,	... *stāso*.
Dat.	*māta*,	to me,	... *mūng ta*.	*tā ta*,	to thee,	... *tāso ta*.
Acc.	*mā*,	me,	... *mūng*.	*tā*,	thee,	... *tāso*.
In.	*mā*,	by me,	... *mūnga*.	*tā*,	by thee,	... *tāso*.
Loc.	*pa mā ke* (*kkhe*)	in me.	... *pa mūnga ke*,	*pa tā ke* (*kkhe*),	in thee.	... *pa tāso ke*,
Abl.	*la mā na*	from me.	... *la mūnga na*,	*la tā na*,	from thee,	... *la tāso na*.
				ai tā,	oh, thou!	... *ai tāso*.

Third Person Proximate.	*Third Person Remote.*
Nom. and Acc. *dā* or *de*, he, she *or* it. plur. *doī.*	*hag̱ha*, he, she *or* it, *hag̱hoī* or *hag̱ho.*
Oblique cases, *da* or *de*, plur. *do* or *doyo.*	Masc. *hag̱huh.* Fem. *hag̱he.*

The following forms are occasionally, though seldom, used. (*See Section I., Phrase* 66) :—

me, me, by me, mine ; plur. *mū*, us, by us, our.
de, thee, by thee, thine ; ... *mū*, you, by you, your.
ye, him, by him, his ; ... *ye*, by them.

With the affixes *ta*, to, *ke* (*k̲h̲he*), in, &c., and also in comp. with verbs, the following are used:—*rā*, me, us ; *dar*, thee, you ; *war*, him, her, it. The affixes are, however, omitted in speaking. (*See Section I., Phrases* 44 *and* 45).

Demonstrative Pronouns.

Nom. and Acc. *dag̱ha* or *dā*, this ; plur. *dag̱hoī* or *de.*
Oblique *dag̱ha* or *da ;* ... *dag̱ho* or *deo.*

The Personal Pronouns *hag̱ha* and *de* are used for 'that': *k̲h̲pul*, 'own,' corresponds to the Hindī *apnā.*

The following compounds are in common use :—"Other one," *bal* (*bul*) *yo*, fem. *bala yuwa ;* "all the rest," *nor ṭol*, fem. *nore ṭole.* "Which one," *kūm yo*, fem. *kuma yuwa ;* "many more," *nor ḍer*, fem. *nore ḍere.* "Every one," *har yo*, fem. *hara yuwa.*—Also, *bul tsok*, "other person ;" *bul tsa*, "other thing :" *nor tsok*, "who else ?" *nor tsa*, "what else ?" *har tsok*, "every body ;" *har tsuh*, "every thing :" *hets tsok na*, "nobody ;" *har tso*, "however many."

The Auxiliary Verb—*Yam*, "I am."

Indicative.				*Subjunctive.* (Sign the Particle *ka* before the Pronoun.)	
Present.		*Future.* I will be, &c.	*Past.* I was, &c.	*Present.* If I be, &c.	*Past.* If I were, &c.
Zuh yam,	I am,	*ba yam*,	*wum*,	*ka zuh wum*,	*wai.*
Tuh ye,	Thou art,	*ba ye*,	*we*,	*we*,	*wai.*
Hag̱ha dai,	He is,	*ba wī*,	*wuh*,	*wī*,	*wai.*
Hag̱ha dah,	She is,	*ba wī*,	*wah*,	*wī*,	*wai.*
Mūng yū,	We are,	*ba yū*,	*wū*,	*wū*,	*wai.*
Tāso yai,	You are,	*ba yai*,	*waī*,	*waī*,	*wai.*
Hag̱hoè dè,	They are,	*ba wī*,	*wū*,	*wī*,	*wai.*

The Intransitive Auxiliary Verb—*Kedal*, "to become."

Indicative Mood.

Present.		*Future.* I shall become, &c.	*Imperfect.* I was becoming, &c.
Kegam,	I become,	*ba kegam*,	*kedalam* or *kedam*.
Kege,	Thou becomest,	*ba kege*,	*kedale* or *kede*.
Kegī,	He becomes,	*ba kegī*,	*keduh*, fem. *kedala*, *kedah*.
Kegū,	We become,	*ba kegū*,	*kedalū*, *kedū*.
Kegaī,	You become,	*ba kegaī*,	*kedalaī*, *kedaī*.
Kegī,	They become,	*ba kegī*,	*kedal*, fem. *kedale*.

Gerund, *kedūn*, fem., *kedana*, "the becoming."
Present Part., *keduh*, fem. *kedala*, "becoming."
Active Part., or Noun of Agency, *kedunkai*, (fem. ī), "a becomer."

The Intransitive Auxiliary Verb—*Shwal*, "to become," *or* "to be."

Indicative Mood.

Present.		*Imperfect.* I was becoming,	*Perfect.* I have become.
Sham,	I become,	*shwalam*,	*shawai yam*.
She,	Thou becomest,	*shwale*,	*shawai ye*.
Shī,	He becomes,	*shwuh* or *shuh*,	*shawai dai*.
	(fem.)	*shwala* or *shwah*,	*shawī dah*.
Shū or *shwū*,	We become,	*shwalū*,	*shawī yū*.
Shaī,	You become,	*shwaloī*,	*shawī yaī*.
Shī,	They become,	*shwal* or *shū*,	*shawī dī*.
	(fem.)	*shwale* or *shwe*,	

The Subjunctive Mood forms its Tenses by prefixing *ka*, "if," to the Tenses of the Indicative Mood.

Tenses formed from the Present:—Aorist, by the prefix *wu*. Future, by *wu ba;* or, if the Pers. pronoun is used, *ba wu*, as *zuh ba wu sham*, I shall become.

The Past is formed from the Imperfect, by the prefix *wu*.

The Pluperfect from the Perfect:—*Shawai wum*, ... *we*, ... *wuh*, fem. *wah; shawī wū*, ... *waī*, ... *wū*.

Doubtful Future, *ba wum*, &c.

Gerund, *shwūn*, fem. *shwana*, "the becoming."

Pres. Part., *shwal*, fem. *shwala*, "becoming."

Active Part., or Noun of Agency, *shwunkai* or *shwunai*, "becomer."

Pass. Part., *shwalai* or *shawai*, "become."

Transitive Verb.

Active Voice—*wahal*, "to strike."

Indicative Present—I strike, thou strikest, &c.

Sing. *waham, wahe, wahī;* Plur. *wahū, wahaī, wahī.*

Aorist—I may strike, &c., *wu waham, wu wahe*, &c.

Future—I shall strike, &c., *wu ba waham*, &c., or, with Pronoun, *zuh ba wu waham*, &c.

The Imperfect, Past, Perfect and Pluperfect require the Agent Case instead of the Nominative, and the Verb agrees with the object.

The Imperfect.

Thou, you, he, she, it *or* they,	was (were) striking me	*tā tāso, haghuh* or *hagho*	*zuh wahalam.*
... ...	... us	...	*mūng wahalū.*
I, we, he, she, it *or* they,	was (were) striking thee	*mā mūng, haghuh* or *hagho*	*tā wahale.*
... ...	... you	...	*tāso wahalaī.*
I, we, thou *or* you,	was (were) striking him / her	*mā mūng, tā* or *taso*	*hagha* *wahuh.* / *wahala.*
... ...	them / them (fem.)	...	*haghoī* *wahal.* / *wahale.*

The Perfect.

Thou, you, he, she, it *or* they,	has (have) struck me	*tā tāso, haghuh* or *hagho*	*zuh wahalai yam.*
... ...	us	...	*mūng wahali yū.*

And, similarly:—

...	has or have struck thee,	*tuh wahalai ye.*
...	... you,	*tāso wāhalī yaī.*
...	... him *or* her,	*hagha wahalai dah.*
...	... them,	*haghoe wahalī dī.*
	them (fem.)	*haghe wahalī dī.*

The Past is formed from the Imperfect by prefixing *wu:—tā zuh wu wahalam*, "thou didst strike me."

The Continuative Past is formed thus:—*Mā ba hagha wāhuh*, "I used to strike him."

The Pluperfect thus:—*Mā hagha wahalai wuh*, "I had struck him."

The Doubtful Pluperfect:—*Hagha ba zuh wahalai yam*, "He might have struck me."

The Imperative:—"Strike," *wu waha;* Plur. *wu wahaī.*
"Let him strike," *wu de wahī; ...* *wu de wahī.*

The Subjunctive Mood is formed by prefixing *ka,* "if," to the Indicative.

The Potential Mood, corresponding to the use of *sakna* in Urdū, is formed from the Past Part.; the Present with the Present of *shwal* thus,—

Wahalai sham, "I can strike;" *wahalai she,* "thou canst strike;" *wahalai shū,* "we can strike," &c.

In the Past the Verb agrees with the object, as in the past tenses of the Indicative:—

Thou, you, he, she, it *or* they	could have struck me,	*tā tāso hagha* or *hagho*	*zuh wahalai shwam.*
...	... ... us,	... ...	*mūng wahalī shurī.*
I, we, he, she, it *or* they	could have struck thee,	*mā, mūng hagha* or *hagho*	*tuh wahalai shwe.*
...	... ... you,	... ...	*tāso wahalī shwaī.*
I, we, thou *or* you	... ... him	*mā mūng*	*haghawahalaishuh.*
	her	*tā* or *tāso*	*hagha wahalī shwa.*
...	... ... them	... ...	*haghoī wahalī shwal (shwū).*
...	... them (fem.)		*haghoī wahalī shwe.*

The change of termination of the Verb itself,—*wahalai*—according to the gender of the object is a curious anomaly, and some Grammarians say it is impossible, but the Afghāns certainly give the inflection.

The Potential Future is formed with *ba,* as *zuh ba tlai sham,* I shall be able to go.

Gerund:—*wahūn,* fem. *wahana,* "striking;"
Pres. Part., *wahuh,* fem. *wahala,* "striking;"
Noun of Agency:—*wahunkai* or *wahunai,* "a striker;"
Past Part., *wahalai,* fem. *wahalī,* "struck."

Passive Voice.

Wahalai kedal, "to be struck."

The Passive Voice is formed by conjugating the Past Participle with the auxiliaries *kedal* and *shwal,* and making the usual changes for number, gender, and person.

Gerund, *wahalai keduh;* Past. Part., *wahalai shawai.*

Indicative Mood.

Singular.	Present.	Imperfect. I was being struck.	Perfect. I have been struck.
I am struck,	*wahalai kegam,*	*wahalai kedam,*	*wahalai shawai yam.*
Thou art struck,	... *kege*	... *kede,*	... ... *ye.*
He is struck,	... *kegī,*	... *keduh,*	... ... *dai.*
She is struck,	*wahalī kegī,*	*wahalī* { *kedah,* *kedala.*	*wahalī shāwī dah.*
Plural.			
We are struck,	*wahalī kegū,*	*wahalī kedū,*	*wahalī shawī yū.*
You are struck,	... *kegaī,*	... *kedaī,*	... ... *yaī.*
They are struck,	... *kegī,*	... *kedal,* fem.... *kedale.*	... ... *dī.*

Tenses formed from the Present:—Aorist, *wu wahalai kegam.* Future, *wahalai ba kegam ;* as *zuh ha wahalai kegam.*

Tenses from the Imperfect:—Past, *wu wahalai,* "I was struck." Continuative Past, *wahalai ba kegam,* or *zuh ba wahalai kegam.*

Tenses from the Perfect:—Pluperfect, *wahalai shawai wum,* "I had been struck." Doubtful future, *wahalai shawai ba wam,* or *zuh ba wahalai shawai wam.*

Imperative Mood.

Wahalai sha, "be struck;" Plur. *wahalī shaī.*
Hag̱ha de wahalai shī, "let him be struck;" ... *hag̱hoī de wahalī shī.*
Fem. ... *wahalī shī* "let her be struck."

THE INTRANSITIVE VERB.—*Khwazedal,* "to move."

Indicative.

Sing.	Present.	Imperfect.	Past.	Perfect.
1 pers.	*k̲h̲wazegam,*	*k̲h̲wazedalam,*	*wu k̲h̲wazedam,*	*k̲h̲wazedalai yam*
2 pers.	*k̲h̲wazege,*	*k̲h̲wazedale,*	*wu k̲h̲wazede,*	... ... *ye.*
3 masc.	*k̲h̲wazegī,*	*k̲h̲wazeduh,*	*wu k̲h̲wazeduh,*	... ... *dai.*
3 fem.		*k̲h̲waze-* { *dah,* *dala,*	*wu k̲h̲waze-* { *dah,* *dala*	*k̲h̲wazedalī dah.*
Plur.				
1 pers.	*k̲h̲wazegū,*	*k̲h̲wazedalū,*	*wu k̲h̲wazedū,*	*k̲h̲wazedalī yū.*
2 pers.	*k̲h̲wazegaī,*	*k̲h̲wazedalai,*	*wu k̲h̲wazedaī,*	... ... *yaī*
3 masc.	*k̲h̲wazegī,*	*k̲h̲wazedal,*	*wu k̲h̲wazedal,*	... ... *dī.*
3 fem.		*k̲h̲wazedale,*	*wu k̲h̲wazedale,*	

Tenses formed from the Present:—Aorist, *wu k̲h̲wazegam.* Future, *wu ba k̲h̲wazegam.*

From the Past:—The Continuative Past, *k̲h̲wazedam ba.*

From the Perfect:—Pluperfect, *wum,* &c. Doubtful, *ba wum,* &c.

Imperative.

Sing., *wu khwazega*, "move;" plur, *wu khwazegaī*.
wu de khwazegī, "let him move;" ... *wu de khwazegī*.

Gerund, *khwazedūn*, "a moving;"
Pres. Part., *khwazeduh*, "moving."
Noun of Agency, *khwazedūnkai*, "a mover;"
Past Part., *khwazedalai*, "having moved."

Potential.

Present, *khwazedalai sham*, &c.
Past, *khwazedalai shwam*, &c.
Future, *khwazedalai ba sham*, &c.

THE TRANSITIVE AUXILIARY—*Kawul*, "to do."

Indicative.—Present.

	Singular.	*Plural.*
I do,	*kawam* or *kṛam*	*kawū* or *kṛū*.
Thou dost,	*kawe*, or *kṛe*	*kawaī* or *kṛaī*.
He does,	*kawī*, *kṛī* or *kānde*	*kawī*, *krī* or *kānde*.

Imperfect.

In agreement with the objects in number and gender:

Masc. *Mā tā*, &c. *kawuh*; plur. *kawal*.
Fem. *kawala*; ... *kawale*.

The Future is formed by prefixing *ba* to the Present:—*zah ba kaṛam*, &c.

Imperative.

Sing. Do thou, *wu kṛa* or *wu ka*; plur. *wu kṛaī* or *wu kaī*.
Let him do, *hagha de wuh ka*; ... *hagha de wu kṛī* or *kānde*.

Subjunctive.—Present.

Singular.	*Plural.*
If I do, *ka kawam*,	*ka kawū*.
If thou doest, *ka kawe*,	*ka kawaī*.
If he does, *ka kawī*,	*ka kawī* or *kānde*.

Past.

Masc.	*ka kaṛai wai*,	*ka kaṛī wai*.
Fem.	*ka kaṛī waī*,	*ka kaṛī wai*.

(*See Phrase* 62, *Section I.*)

The Future Subjunctive is formed by prefixing *ba*, as *ka ba wu kaṛam* (or *kam*), &c.

The Irregular Verbs in Pashtū are very difficult, and it would be useless to attempt any explanation of them in this Work.

For the Numerals, see end of "Elements of Persian Grammar," page 20.

PART II.

SENTENCES.

Note.—In most of the Phrases one word is printed in italics, in each of the four languages, to assist the student in picking out rapidly the equivalents of the several English words; for instance, in Section I., Phrase 2, it is seen at once that *boy* is in Hindustani, *laṛka;* in Persian, *ṭifl;* and in Pashtū, *halak.* Again, in Section I., Phrase 28, it is seen that *has he* must in this and similar phrases be rendered in Hindustani by *us ke pās hain*, and in Pashtū by *da haghuh dzakha dī*, both of which mean, "*are in his possession.*" By this means the idiomatic translation of the English expression is shown instead of only the literal, which is all that can be given in a Vocabulary. For this reason the words given in the Vocabulary, in many cases, differ from those given in this Part.

SECTION I.—NOUNS AND VERBS.

English.	*Urdū.*	*Persian.*	*Pashtū.*
1 This *man* is my brother.	Yih *ādmī* merā *bhāī* hai.	Īn *shakhṣ* barādar i man ast.	Dā *sarai* dzamā wror dai.
2 That *boy* is your son.	Wuh *laṛkā* tumhārā betā hai.	Ān *tifl* pisar i shumā ast.	Hagha *halak* stā zoe dai.
3 These are their *houses*.	Ye unke *ghar* haiṅ.	Īn khānahā e eshān and.	Dā *korūnā* da hagho dī.
4 This is my *father's* field.	Yih mere *bāp kā* khet hai.	Īn zarā'at *az padar* i man ast.	Dā paṭai dzamā *da plār* dai.
5 That woman was my *sister*.	Wuh 'aurat merī *bahin* thī.	Ān zan *khwāhir* i man būd.	Hagha khaza dzamā *khor* wah.
6 *His* brother was my father.	*Us kā* bhāī merā bāp thā.	Barādar *i o* padar i man būd.	*Da haghuh* wror dzamā plār wuh.
7 My *uncle* is his *grandfather*.	Merā *chachā* uskā *dādā hai.*	*'Ammū* i man *jad* i o ast (*pronounced* ost).	Dzamā *truh* da haghuh *nikuh* dai.
8 His sister is my *wife*.	Uskī bahin merī *jorū* hai.	Hamshīra i o *zoja* i man ast.	Da haghuh khor dzamā *khaza* dah.
9 Your brother's *horse* is swift *and* my father's *elephant* is slow.	Tumhare bhāī kā *ghoṛā* tezrau hai *aur* hamāre bāp kā *hāthī* sust hai.	*Asp* i barādar i shumā tezrau ast *wa fīl* i padar i man sust.	Stā da wror *ās* chābak dai *au* dzamā da plār *āthī* sust dai.
10 Your sister is *handsome, but* her son is *ugly*.	Tumhārī bahin *khūbsūrat* hai *lekin* uskā beṭā *bad ṣūrat* hai.	Khwāhir i shumā *khūbrū ast magar* pisar ash *badshakl* ast.	Stā khor *pāe makhe* dah *wale* da haghe zoi ḍer *bad rang* dai.
11 His father is *taller* than his brother.	Us kā bāp uske bhāī se *lanbā* hai.	Padar i o az barādar ash *bu-landtar* ast.	Da haghuh plār da haghuh la wror na *lwaṛ* dai.
12 The *cow* is shorter than the horse.	*Gāī* ghoṛe se ḳadd meṅ chhoṭī hai.	*Gāo* az asp khurdtar ast.	*Ghwā* la ās na wāṛa dah.
13 *Cloth* is thicker than *paper*.	*Kapṛā kāghaz* se moṭā hai.	*Pārcha* az *kāghaz* (purkārtar) luktar ast.	*Khamtā la kāghaz* na ghaṭa dah.

English.	Urdū.	Persian.	Pashtū.
14 That *antelope* is the swiftest.	Wuh *hiran* sab se tezrau hai.	An *āhū* tēztarīn ast.	Hagha *osai* la tolo na gaṛandai dai.
15 Who is that *man?*	Wuh kaun *ādmī* hai?	Ān kudām *shakhṣ* ast?	Hagha kūm *saṛai* dai?
16 Who is that *woman?*	Wuh kaun *'aurat* hai?	O kudām *zan* ast?	Hagha kūma *khāza* dah?
17 Whose is this *book?*	Yih *kitāb* kiskī hai?	Īn *kitāb* az kīst?	Dā *kitāb* da chā dai?
18 To whom did he *give* the *hat?*	Usne *topī* kis ko *dī?*	O *kulāh* ba ki *dād?*	Haghuh *ṭopai* chāta *warkṛa?*
19 Is his *wife* handsome?	Kyā, us kī *jorū* khūbṣūrat hai?	Ahl i *khāna* ash khūb ṣūrat ast?	Da haghuh *khaza* khhāyastah dah?
20 How many *tables* are there?	Kitnī *mezeṅ* haiṅ?	Chand tā *mezhā* hastand?	Tsomra *mezūnā* dī?
21 How many *stones* are there in the house?	Us ghar meṅ kitne *pathar* haiṅ?	Dar ān khāna chi ḳadar *sang* ast?	Pa haghuh kor ke tsomra *kāṅṛī* dī?
22 What sort of *boots* are they?	We kaise *moze* haiṅ?	Ān *mozahā* chi ṭaur hastand?	Hagha tsa ranga *paṅṛe* dī?
23 *He lives* on the mountain.	*Wuh* pahāṛ ke ūpar *rahtā.*	O bala e koh *mīmānad.*	*Hagha* pa ghrah bānde *osī.*
24 They walk under the *bridge.*	We *pul* ke nīche jāte haiṅ.	Eshān zer i *pul* mīrawand.	Haghoī da *pul* lānde dzī.
25 They come from the *city; where* do you come from?	We *shahr* se āte; tum *kahāṅ se* āte ho?	Eshān az *shahr* miāyand shumā az *kujā* miāyed?	Haghoī la *khahra* na rāzī tāso la *kūm dzāī* na rāzai?
26 A hat is on his *head.*	Us ke *sir* par topī hai.	Bālāe *sar* ash kullāh ast.	Da haghuh pa *sar* ṭopaī dah.
27 A stick is in his *hand.*	Us ke *hāth* meṅ lāṭhī hai.	Ba *dast* i o chob ast.	Da haghuh pa *lās* ke yau largaī dai.
28 How many rupees *has he?*	*Us ke pās* kitne rūpaie *haiṅ?*	*O* chand rūpīya *mīdārad?*	*Da haghuh dzakha* tsomra rūpaī *dī.*
29 How many horses *does* she *keep?*	Wuh kitne ghoṛe *rakhtī* hai?	O chand asp *dārad?*	*Da* haghe dzakha tsomra āsūna *dī.*
30 *I send* my son.	*Maiṅ* apne laṛke ko *bhejtā hūṅ.*	*Man* pisar i khud [written khūd] rā *mīfaristam.*	*Zuh* khpul zoe *legam.*

English.	Urdū.	Persian.	Pashtū.
31 He *beats* his servant.	Wuh apne naukar ko *mārtā hai.*	O mulāzim i khud rā *mīzanad.*	Hagha khpul naukar *wahī.*
32 We *bring* our sheep.	Ham apne bheṛ *lāte* haiṅ.	Mā gospindān i khud *mīārem.*	Mūng khpule gade *rāwalū.*
33 You *drink* water.	Tum pānī *pīte ho.*	Shumā āb *mīnoshed.*	Tāsu obuh *tskaī.*
34 They *eat* meat.	We gosht *khāte haiṅ.*	Ānān gosht *mīkhurand.*	Haghoī ghwakha *khurī.*
35 I saw your *goat.*	Maiṅ ne tumhārī *bakrī* dekhī.	Man *buz* i shumā dīda am.	Mā da tā *wzah* wulī dah.
36 He *bought* my horse.	Us ne merā ghoṛā *mol-liyā.*	O asp i marā *kharīd.*	Haghuh dzamā ās *wākhast.*
37 We *threw* stones.	Ham ne pathar *pheṅke.*	Mā sanghā *andākhtem.*	Mūng kānṛī *wughurzawal.*
38 They *picked up* a rope.	Un ne ek rassī *uṭhāī.*	Ānān yak respān *bardāshtand.*	Haghoī yau puṛai *porta kuh.*
39 I killed the *hare.*	Maiṅ ne *khar-gosh* ko mārā.	Man *khar-gosh* rā kushtam.	Mā *soya* mṛah kṛah.
40 They *stole* the horse.	Unhoṅ ne ghoṛā *churāyā.*	Eshān asp rā *ba duzdī burdand.*	Haghoe ās *pa ghla bot.*
41 I shall give a *coat* to him.	Maiṅ ek *kurtā* use dūṅgā.	Man *farghale* ba o khwāham dād.	Zuh ba haghuh ta yuwah khalka warkṛam.
42 He will give me a *gun.*	Wuh ek *bandūk* mujh ko degā.	O yak *tufang* mārā khwāhad dād.	Hagha ba mā ta yau *ṭupak* rākṛī.
43 We shall take a *pistol* from him.	Ham ek *pistol* us se leṅge.	Mā yak *tufang-cha* az o khwāhem girift.	Mūng ba la haghuh na yuwa *tamāncha* wākhlū.
44 You *will go* to him.	Tum uske pās jāoge.	Shumā ba nizd i o *khwāhed raft.*	Tāso ba war *zaī.*
45 Will they come to us?	We hamāre pās āweṅge?	Eshān pesh i mā khwāhand āmad?	Haghoe ba rā la rāshī?
46 I *have smelt* the water.	Maiṅ ne pānī ko *sūnghā* hai.	Man ābrā *boīda am.*	Mā obuh *boī kaṛī dī.*
47 He has *cut* a stick.	Us ne ek lakṛī *kātī* hai.	O chob i dastī *burīda* ast.	Hagha yau largai pre *kaṛai* dai.
48 We have *built* a house.	Ham ne ek makān *banāyā* hai.	Mā yak makān *sākhta* em.	Mūng yau kor *jor kaṛai dai.*

English.	Urdū.	Persian.	Pashtū.
49 You have *cleaned* the gun.	Tum ne bandūḳ ko *ṣāf kiya* hai.	Shumā tufang rā *ṣāf karda ed.*	Tāso ṭopak *ṣāf kaṛai dai.*
50 They have dried the *clothes.*	Unhoṅ ne *kapṛoṅ* ko sukhāyā hai.	Anān *jāmahā* rā khushk karda and.	Hagho *jāme* wuche kaṛī dī.
51 I had washed my *face.*	Maiṅ ne apnā *muṅh* dhoyā thā.	Man *rūe* khud rā shusta būd-am.	Mā khpul *mukh* wīṅzalai wuh.
52 He had *scratched* his hand.	Usne apnā hāth *chhīlā thā.*	O dast i khud rā *kharāshīda* būd.	Hagha khpul lās *ghuts kaṛai* wuh.
53 We had split the *root.*	Ham ne us *jaṛ* ko chīrā thā.	Mā ān *bekh* rā shigāfta būd-em.	Mā hagha *wulī* tsīralī wah.
54 Had you gathered the *flowers?*	Tum ne *phūl* toṛe the?	Shumā *gulhā* chīda būded?	Tā *gulūnā* āṅṛawulī wū?
55 They *had shaken* the tree.	Unhoṅ ne peṛ ko *hilāyā thā.*	Eshān darakht rā *jumbānīda būdand.*	Haghoe wunah *tsandawalī wah.*
56 *If* I plane the table it *will become* smooth.	*Jo* maiṅ mez ko rande se ṣāf karūṅ to wuh chiknā *hojāegā.*	*Agar* mez rā ba randa ṣāf kunam hamwār *khẉāhad shud.*	*Ka* zuh mez pa rande sara ṣāf kṛam hamwār *ba shī.*
57 If *it rains* to-morrow the *foot-path* will be slippery.	Jo kal *pānī paṛegā* to *pagdandī* meṅ phislan hojāegā.	Agar fardā *bārān shawad* dar *rāh* laghzānī khẉāhad shud.	Ka ṣabā *bārān shī lār* ba khuwana ṣhī.
58 If we get thirsty we shall drink *wine.*	Jo ham ko piyās lagegā to *sharāb* pieṅge.	Agar mā tishna shawem *sharāb* khẉāhem khūrd (*more correct*, noshīd).	Ka mūng tagī shū *sharāb* ba tskū.
59 If you are *hungry*, eat *now.*	Jo tum *bhūkhe* ho, to *ab* khāo.	Agar shumā *gurisna* ed *hālā* bukhūred.	Ka tāso *wagī* yaī, no *os* wukhuṛaī.
60 If our *feet* slip we *shall fall.*	Jo hamāre *pāṅw* phisal jāeṅge to ham *gir paṛeṅge.*	Agar *pāe* mā bi laghzad mā *khẉāhem uftād.*	Ka dza mūng *pkhe* wukhoigī no *ba prewzū.*

English.	Urdū.	Persian.	Pashtū.
61 If I *had heard* him I should have *answered.*	Jo maiṅ usko *suntā* to *jawāb detā.*	Agar man sukhan i o ra *mīshunīdam jawāb* asl *mīdādam.*	Ka mā auredilai wai *dzawāb* ba *me warkaṛai wuh.*
62 If he *had seen* you he would have told me.	Jo wuh tum ko *dekhtā* to wuh mujh se kahtā.	Agar shumārā *mīdīd* ba man mīguft.	Ka hagha tuh *līdalaī* wai mā ta ba ye welī wū.
63 If we had gone to Peshawur we should have *also* gone to Cherat.	Jo ham Peshāwar ko jāte to ham Cherāt ko *bhī* jāte.	Agar ba Peshāwar mīraftem ma ba Cherāt *ham* mīraftem.	Ka mūng Pekhaur ta talī wai no Cherat la ba *ham* talī wū.
64 If you had *fired* the gun you would have killed a *fox.*	Jo tum bandūḳ *chalāte* to ek *lomṛī* mārte.	Agar shumā tufang rā *sar mīkarded* yak *robah* mī kushted.	Ka tā ṭopak *khlās karai* wai no yuwah soyā ba de wīsh tālī wah.
65 If they had *polished* the scimitars they would have shone.	Agar we talwār *ṣaiḳal karte* to chamaktīṅ.	Agar eshān shamsherahā rā *ṣaiḳal mī kardand* barrāḳ mīshudand (*or,* mīdarakhshand).	Ka haghoī tūre *ṣaiḳal kaṛī wah* no ba zalī dī.
66 If I *had* not *scraped* the *bark* off it would not have withered.	Agar maiṅ uskā *post* na *chhīltā* to wuh na murjhātā.	Agar *post* i ān rā na *mī tarāshīdem* pazhmurda na mīshud.	Ka da haghuh *postakai* me bel kaṛai na wai no muṛ shawai ba na wuh.
67 If he had not pierced a *hole* in it the water would not have run out.	Agar wuh usmeṅ *chhed* na kartā to pānī na bahtā.	Agar o dar ān *surākh* na karde ābash na rekhte.	Ka haghuh pa haghuh ke *sūrai* kaṛai na wai obuh ba na bahī dī.
68 If you did not *formerly* do *bricklayer's work,* what did you do?	Agar tum *peshtar rājgīrī* na karte the to, kyā karte the?	Agar shumā *peshtar mī' mārī* ne mī karded chi mīkarded?	Ka tā *wṛānde gilkārī* na kawala no tsuh de kawal?
69 If the *cloth seller* had been present yesterday he would have been *angry.*	Jo *kapṛe wālā* kal ḥāẓir hotā to *khafā* hotā.	Dīroz agar *bazzāz* ḥāẓir mī būd albatta *nārāẓ* mīshud.	Ka parūn *bajāz* ḥāẓir wai *khapa* shawai ba wuh.

English.	*Urdū.*	*Persian.*	*Pashtū.*
70 He *can run* and she can sew.	Wuh *dauṛ saktā* aur wuh sī saktī.	O *dawīdan mī tawānad* wa o dokhtan.	Hagha *zghaledai shī* au hagha gandal kawalī shī.
71 He could kiss the *king's* hand, and she could sing.	Wuh *pādshāh* kā hāth chūm sakā aur wuh gā sākī.	O dast i *bādshāh* rā bosīdan tawānist wa o sarāīdan tawānist.	Hagha da *bādshāh* lās kkhkwalawalai shuh au haghe sandare wayale shwe.
72 The youth could have walked about if he had not been *tired.*	Agar wuh jawān *thakā* na hotā to idhar udhar phir saktā.	Agar ān jawān *māndā* na mī būd albatta sair kardan mī tawānist.	Ka hagha dzwān *staṛai* na wai garzedalai ba shuh.
73 We shall be able to talk about *geometry* and arithmetic.	Ham *'ilm i paimāish* aur ḥisāb par guftgū kar sakeṅge.	Mā ba *'ilm i masāḥat* wa siyāḳat baḥs kardan khwāhem tawānist.	Mūng ba pa *kach* au pa shmār khabare kawalai shū.

SECTION II.—GENERAL ORDERS AND QUESTIONS.

English.	*Urdū.*	*Persian.*	*Pāshtū.*
1 Come *here;* come near.	*Idhar* āo; nazdīk āo.	*Īnjā* biyā; nazdīk biyā.	*Dale* rāsha; nizhde rāsha.
2 Come in; come *back.*	Bhītar āo; *lauṭ* āo.	Darūn biyā; *wāpas* biyā.	Danana rāsha; *bahartā* rāsha.
3 Be silent; be *careful.*	Chup raho; *khabardār* ho.	Khāmosh shau; *khabardār.*	Chup sha; *bedār* sha.

English.	Urdū.	Persian.	Pashtū.
4 Remember; *don't forget.*	Yād rakho; *bhūlo mat.*	Yād dār; *farāmosh makun.*	Yād larā; *herawa ma.*
5 Go away; go *home.*	Chale jāo; *ghar ko* jāo.	Burau; *ba khāna* burau.	Zā; *kor tā* zā.
6 *Make haste;* bring that.	*Jaldī karo;* usko lāo.	*Zūd shau;* ān rā biyār.	*Zar sha;* hagha rāwṛa.
7 Give it to me; *let it alone.*	Mujhe do; *rahne do.*	Marā bidih; *buguzārasa.*	Māla rāka; *pregda.*
8 Open the *door;* shut the door.	*Darwāza* kholo; darwāza band karo.	*Darwāza* rā wā kun; dar rā band kun.	*War* lare kṛa; war pūre kṛa.
9 Light the *lamp.*	*Chirāgh* ko jalāo.	*Chirāgh* rā roshan kun (*or,* biyafroz).	*Ḍīwā* bala ka.
10 Put out the *candle.*	*Battī* bujhāo.	Ḳandīl gul kun.	*Baṭaī* mṛah ka.
11 Get *down* from there.	Wahāṅ se *nīche* utro.	Az ān jā *pāyān* biyā.	La hagh zāī na rā *kūz* shā.
12 Turn to the *right,* then turn to the *left.*	*Dāhine* phiro, tab *bāeṅ* phiro.	Awwal ba dast-i-*rāst* bigard, bāz ba dast-i-*chap.*	Wṛambai *khī* lās ta, bya *guts* lās ta wugarza.
13 *Call* the *cook* and the groom.	*Bāwarchī* aur sāīs *bulāo.*	*Bāwarchī* o sāīs bi-*talab.*	*Ḍodai pakhwūnkai,* au sāīs rā *wubola.*
14 Have patience; *don't bother.*	Ṣabr karo, *diḳḳ mat do.*	Ṣabr kūn, *diḳḳ makun.*	Ṣabr kawa, *ma me tangawa.*
15 Go out of the house *quickly.*	Ghar men se *jaldī* niklo.	Az khānā *zūd* berūn shau.	La kor na *zar* wuwuza.
16 Take this *note* to the *fort.*	Yih *chiṭṭhī ḳil' a ko* lejāo.	Īn *khaṭṭ* rā ba *ḳil'a* bi rasāned.	Dā *khaṭṭ ḳil'e* ta yosa.
17 Bring an *answer.*	*Jawāb* le āo.	*Jawāb* biyār.	*Zawāb* rāwṛa.
18 Don't make a *noise.*	*Ghul* mat karo.	*Shor* ma kun.	*Shor* ma kawa.
19 Do as I say.	Mere kahne ke muwāfiḳ karo.	Ba gúfta i man bikun.	Chi zuh darta wa yam hagha kawa.
20 Mind your own *business.*	Apnā *kām* karo.	*Kār* i khud kun.	Khpal *kār* kawa.
21 What is your *name?*	Tumhārā *nām* kyā hai?	*Nām* i shumā chīst?	*Nūm* de tsuh dai?
22 What *work* are you doing?	Tum kaunsā *kām* karte ho?	Shumā chi *kār* mī kuned?	Tuh tsuh *kār* kawe?

English.	Urdū.	Persian.	Pashtū.
23 Go there; stand up.	Udhar jāo; khaṛā ho jāo.	Ān sū burau; istāda shau.	Halta zā; wuderega.
24 Lie down; sit on the *chair.*	Leṭ jāo; *kursī* par baiṭho.	Darāz shau; bālā i *kursī* bi nishin.	Tsomla; pa *tsaukai* bānde kena.
25 Stand still; what is this?	Khaṛā raho; yih kyā hai?	Istāda bi mān; īn chīst?	Wuderega; dā tsa dī?
26 Where do you come from?	Tum kahāṅ se āe?	Shumā az kujā āmada ed (*or,* az kudām mulk hasted)?	Tuh la kūm dzāī na rāghle?
27 Where do you live? and what does he want?	Tum kahāṅ rahte ho? aur wuh kyā chāhtā hai?	Shumā kujā mī maned? wa o chi mī khwāhad?	Tuh chirta ose? au hagha tsa ghwārī?
28 Where are you going?	Tum kidhar jāte ho?	Shumā kudām sū mī rawed?	Tuh charta ze?
29 Is *any one* there? who is there?	Wahāṅ *koī* hai? wahāṅ kaun hai?	Ānjā *kase* hast? ānjā kīst?	Haltā *tsok* shta? halta tsok dai?
30 Where has he gone? when *will* he *return?*	Wuh kahāṅ gayā? wuh kab *phir āwegā?*	O kujā raft? o bāz kai *khwa-had āmad?*	Hagha charta talai dai? kala *ba* rā *wugarzī?*
31 Do you *recognize* him?	Tum usko *pahchānte* ho?	Shumā orā *mī shināsed?*	Tuh hagha *pezhane?*
32 Is the master *at home?* has he got up? is he *asleep?*	Ṣāhib *ghar meṅ* haiṅ? uṭhe haiṅ? *sote haiṅ?*	Ṣāhib *ba khāna* hastand? be-dār shuda and? *khwāb mī kunand?*	Ṣāhab *pa kor ke* dai? pātse da-lai dai? hagha *oduh dai?*
33 He is *awake;* don't wake him.	Wuh *jāgte* haiṅ; usko mat jagā o.	Eshān *bedār* hastand; eshān rā bedār ma kuned.	Hagha *wīkh* dai; ma ye wikh-awa.
34 What is the good of that?	Us se kyā fāida hai?	Az ān chi fāida ast?	La haghuh na tsa fāida dah? (*or,* sūd dai?)
35 This is of no use.	Yih kisī kām kā nahiṅ.	Īn lāiḳ i hech kār nest (īn nākār ast).	Dā da hets kār na dai.
36 Why do you do *so?*	Tum *aisā* kyūn karte ho?	Shumā chirā *īn ṭaur* mī-kuned?	Tuh dāse wale kawe?

English.	Urdū.	Persian.	Pashtū.
37 What is the matter?	Kyā hūā?	Chi shud?	Tsa wu shwū?
38 Where did you hear this *news?* who told it to you?	Tum ne yih *khabar* kahāṅ sunī? tum se kisne kahī?	Shumā īn *khabar* kujā shunīdaed? wa ba shumā ki gufta?	Tā dā *khabar* pa kūm zāī ke wāwureduh? tā ta chā wu-wai?
39 How did he hear of it?	Us ne yih kis ṭaraḥ sunā?	O īn rā chiṭaur shunīd?	Hagha dā tsaringa wāwreduh?
40 How do you *know* that it is *true?*	Tum kis ṭaraḥ *jānte* ki yih *sach* hai?	Shumā chigūna *mī dāned* ki īn *rāst* ast?	Tuh tsaringa *pohege* chi da *rekhtiyā* dai?
41 What is your *intention?*	Tumhārā *irāda* kyā hai?	Shumā chi *irāda* dāred?	Stā tsuh *nyat* dai?
42 My *advice* is to stop here for the *night.*	Merī *ṣalāḥ* hai ki *rāt* yahāṅ raheṅ.	*Ṣalāḥ* i man īn ast ki *shab* īnjā bāshem.	Dzamā *nyat* dai chi *shpa* dale wukam.
43 Search for it.	Us ko talāsh karo.	Ānrā bijoed.	Hagha wu laṭawa.
44 What do you call this?	Us ko kyā kahte ho?	Īnrā chi mī goed?	De ta tsuh wāye?
45 What kind of man is he?	Wuh kaisā ādmī hai?	Ān chi ṭaur mard ast?	Hagha tsaranga saṛai dai?
46 What news is there *to-day?*	*Āj* kyā khabar hai?	*Imroz* chi khabar ast?	*Nan* tsa khabar dai?
47 Is there any news? No, there is no news.	Kuchh khabar hai? Kuchh khabar nahīṅ.	Kudām khabar ast? Hech khabar nest.	Tsa khabar shta? Na hets khabar nashta.
48 Is it true or *false?*	Yih sach hai yā *jhūṭh?*	Īn rāst ast yā *darogh?*	Dā rekhtiyā ka *daṛogh* dī.
49 Say it *again; speak* loud.	*Phir* kaho; zor se *bolo.*	*Bāz* bigo; ba āwāz i buland *bugo.*	*Bya* wuwāya; pa zor *wuwāya.*
50 Don't *chatter* so; don't tell lies.	Mat *bako;* jhūṭh na bolo.	*Harzagoī* ma kun; darogh mago.	*Jak* ma waha; darogh ma wāya.
51 What *wages* will you take?	Tum kyā *ṭalab* loge?	Shumā chi *tankhwāh* khwāhed girift?	Tā so *mawājib* ākhle?
52 I will do whatever you order.	Maiṅ bamūjib tumhāre ḥukm ke karūṅgā.	Man bamūjib i hukm i ḥuẓūr khwāham kard.	Har tsuh chi tuh wāye zuh ba hagha kawam.

English.	*Urdū.*	*Persian.*	*Pashtū.*
53 How far off is your *native country?*	Tumhārā *waṭan* kitnī dūr hai?	*Waṭan* i shumā chi ḳadar dūr ast?	Stā *waṭan* la de dzāī na tsomrā lare dai?
54 Where is your *family?*	Tumhārā *gharbār ke log* kahāṅ haiṅ?	*Ḳabīla* i shumā kujā ast?	Stā *tabar* charta dai?
55 I want a good servant.	Mujh ko ek achchhā naukar chāhiye.	Marā yak mulāzim i khūb mī bāyad.	Māla yau khuh naukar pa kār dai.
56 Do you *agree?* will you take ten rupees a *month?*	Tum *ḳabūl karte* ho? das rupīya *mahīnā* leoge?	Shumā *rāẓī hasted?* dah rupiya dar *māhā* khwāhed girift?	Tuh rāzī ye, tuh las rupya de *miyāshte* ba ākhle?
57 Very good, sir, I agree.	Bahut achchhā ṣāḥib, maiṅ ḳabūl kartā hūṅ.	Bisyār khūb ṣāḥib, rāẓī am.	Kha sāḥiba, zuh rāẓi yam.
58 What are your *commands?*	Āp kā kyā *ḥukm* hai?	*Ḥukm* i wālā chīst?	*Ḥukm* de tsuh dai?
59 I have engaged him as my *servant.*	Ham ne usko *naukar* rakhā hai?	Mā o rā ba *mulāzimat* girifta am.	Mā hagha *naukar* kaṛai dai.
60 Why did you not come *earlier?*	Tum *is se āge* kyūn na āye?	Chirā *peshtar* niyāmaded?	Tuh *wṛānde* wale rānaghle?
61 Has the *washerwoman* come to-day?	Āj *dhobī* āyā hai?	Imroz *gāẓar* amada ast?	Nan *dobī* rāghalai dai?
62 Has the cook returned *yet* from market?	Bāwarchī *abtak* bāzār se phir āyā?	*Tā hāl* bāwarchī az bāzār bāz āmada ast?	Ḍoḍai pakhawūnkai *tar osa* pore la bāzār na rāgarze dai?
63 Let me know when he comes.	Jab wuh āwe hameṅ khabar do.	Har waḳt ki bi āyad mārā khabar kun.	Kūm wakht chi rāshī mā khabar ka.
64 Have my *things* come yet?	Hamāre *asbāb* āyē haiṅ?	*Asbāb* i mā āmada ast?	Zmūng *asbāb* raghalai dai?
65 They *promised to send* them to-day.	Unkā *wa'da* āj *bhejne* kā *thā.*	Eshān *wa'da* i faristādan imroz *karda būdand.*	Da haghoī *wāda* dah chi nan ba ye *rāstawi.*

English.	*Urdū.*	*Persian.*	*Pashtū.*
66 Open this *box* and *empty* it. Put *all* the things in and shut it up.	Is *sandūķ* ko khol kar *khālī karo. Tamām* asbāb us meṅ rakh kar band karo.	Īn *sandūķ* rā kushāda khālī *kun. Tamām* asbāb dar ān nihāda band ash kun.	Dā *sandūķ* parānaza tash ye ka. *Tol* asbāb pa ke kegda, au band ye ka.
67 Lock it and bring the *key*.	Tālā band karkar *kunjī* le āo.	Ķufl rā band karda *kalīd* biyār.	Jandrā band kṛa *kunjī* rāwṛa.
68 Have you lit the *candles?*	Tum ne *baṭti* jalāī?	Shumā *kaṅdīlahā* roshan karda ed?	Tā *bataī* bale kaṛī dī?
69 *Has* the groom *fed* the horse?	Sāīs ne ghoṛe ko *chārā dīyā hai?*	Sāīs asp rā *kāh wa dāna dāda ast?*	Sāīs ās lā *wākhuh dāna warkaṛī dī?*
70 See that all the doors are *shut.*	Dekho ki sab darwāze *band* haiṅ.	Bibīned ki hama darwāzahā *band* bāshand.	Wugora chi tol i darwāze *pūre* dī.
71 Call two punkha *coolies* for the *night*, and two for the *day.*	Do pankhā *ķulī rāṭ* ke, wāsṯe aur do *din* ke wāsṯe bulāo	Barāe bādkash do *ķulī* barāe *shab*, wā do barāe *roz* bi ṯalbed.	Da pakī *mazdūrān* rāwubola dwah da *wraze* da pāra au dwah da *shpe* da pāra.
72 That will do; you may go now.	Bas, ab tum jāo.	Bas, shumā rukhṣat shawed.	Bas, ta os zā.
73 Bring a *shade* for the candle.	Batti ke wāsṯe *fānūs* lāo.	Barāe ķandīl *fānūs* biyār.	Da dīwuṭ da pāra *panūs* rāwṛạ.
74 Clean my *shoes* and put my book on the *shelf.*	Merī *jūtiyāṅ* ṣafa karo aur kitāb *takhte* par rakh do.	*Pāeposh* i man ṣāf kuned wa kitāb bālā e *takhta* binihed.	Dzamā *paiṅṛe* pāke kṛa au kitābūna me pa *ṯāķ* kegda.
75 Have you got my *bed* ready?	Tum ne hamārā *palang* taiyār kīyā?	Shumā *palang* am taiyār karda ed?	Tā dzamā *kaṭ* joṛ kaṛaī dai?
76 Fasten the door and open the *window.*	Darwāza band karo aur *khiṛki* kholo.	Dawāza rā band kun o *darīcha* rā wā kun.	War pore ka, *kiṛkaī* prānaza.

English.	Urdū.	Persian.	Pashtū.
77 Are you at leisure? it is of no *consequence*.	Tumko furṣat hai? kuchh *parwā* na.	Shumā rā furṣat ast? hech *muẓāyaḳa* nest.	Tuh wuzgār ye? dā hets *kha-bara* na dah.
78 Bring my clothes, I will go out.	Hamare kapṛe lao, ham bāhar jāeṅge.	Jāmahā am biyār ki man berūn mī rawam.	Dzamā zaṛūkī rāwṛā zuh ba bāhar zam.
79 Give me the *warm* clothes and the *turban*.	Ham ko *garm* kapṛe aur *pagṛī* do.	Mārā jāmahā i *garm* wa' *dastār* bidih.	*Garmẹ* jāme au *pagṛai* rāka.
80 Do not go there again.	Wahāṅ phir mat jāo.	Ānjā bāz ma rau.	Halta byā ma za.
81 Go straight *forward*.	Sīdhe *āge* ko chalo.	Rāst *pesh* burau.	Mukhā mukh pa *wṛānde* za.
82 Wake me *very early*.	Hamko *baṛī fajr* jagāo.	Mārā *'ala ul ṣabāḥ* bedār kun.	Mā *pa loe saḥar* wikh ka.
83 *Sprinkle* some water on the *ground*.	*Zamīn* par thoṛā pānī *chiṛko*.	Āb bālā e *zamīn bipāsh*.	Obuh pa *zmuke* bānde *chaṛkāo ka*.
84 Bring some water that I may wash my hands and face.	Muṅh hāth dhone ka pānī lāo.	Āb barāe shustan i dast o rū biyār.	Obuh lās o mukh windzo da pārā rāwṛā.
85 He is very *intelligent*.	Wuh bahut *hoshyār* hai.	O bisyār *zīrak* ast.	Hagha ḍer *hokhiyār* dai.
86 Put those rupees in the bag, and *hang* the bag on a peg.	We rupaie ṭhailī meṅ rakh kar, khūntī men *latkāo*.	Ān rupiya rā dar kīsa nihāda ān rā bālā *i* mekh *biyā-wezān*.	Ḥagha rūpaī pa telaī ke wā-chawa au telaī pa maugī bānde *kegda*.
87 Come back this way.	Is raste lauṭ ā o.	Az hamīn rāh wāpas biyā.	Pa de lāre rāwugarza.
88 Move a little *slower*.	Zarra *āhista* chalo.	Ḳadare *āhista tar* burau.	*La de na* lug *roro* zā.
89 Take off my boots and give me a *pillow*.	Hamāre moze (būṭ) utāro aur hamko *takya* do.	Mozahā e mārā bikash wa mārā *bālish* bidih.	Moze me wubāsa au *balikht* rāka.
90 There is no *oil* in the lamp.	Chirāgh meṅ *tel* nahīṅ.	Chirāgh be *raughan* ast.	Pa dīwe ke *tel* nashta.
91 This is a mere *trick*.	Yih ṣirf *fareb* hai.	In ṣirf *fareb* ast.	Dā ṣirf *fareb* dai.
92 Is his *shop* in the "Chauk?"	Uskī *dukān* chauk meṅ hai?	*Dukānash* ba chauk ast?	Da haghuh *dukān* pa chauk ke dai?

English.	Urdū.	Persian.	Pashtū.
93 Bring a rope and tie up the *dog*.	Rassī lākar *kutte* ko bānḍho.	Respān biyār o *sag* rā basta kun.	Paṛai rāwṛa au *spai* wutaṛa.
94 Give me the *tooth-brush* and tooth-powder.	Ham ko *miswāk* aur manjan do.	Mārā *miswāk* o dandān sho (misī) bidih.	*Miswāk* au manjan rāka.
95 Have you a *new* suit of clothes?	Tumhāre pās *naiyā* joṛā kapṛā hai? [do.	Shumā yak jora e jāmahāe *nau* dāred?	Tuh yuwa joṛā da *nawwī* rākht lare?
96 Give me my hat and *whip*.	Hamko ṭopī aur *korā* (chābuk)	Mārā kulāh o *ḳamchī* bidih.	Zuh ṭopaī au *chābuk* ghwāṛam.
97 This rupee is *bad*.	Yih rupīya *khoṭā* hai.	Īn rupīya *ḳalb* ast.	Dā rupaī *kalpa* dah.
98 Its shape and *colour* are wrong.	Uskā shakl aur *rang* nā durust hai.	Shakl wa *rangash* nā durust ast.	Da haghe shekl au *rang* khuh na dai.
99 This is a *difficult* business.	Yih kām *mushkil* hai.	Īn kār *mushkil* ast.	Dā *grān* kār dai.
100 They are great *scoundrels*.	We baṛe *badma'āsh* hain.	Eshān bisyār *badma'āsh* hastand.	Haghoī ḍer *badkār* dī.
101 This cloth is very coarse, I want some *finer*.	Yih kapṛā bahut moṭā hai, *is se mahīn* chāhiye.	Īn jāma bisyār purkār (luk) ast, *bārīktar* bāyad.	Hagha khamtā ḍera ghaṭa dah, zuh bārīka ghwāṛam.
102 How *long* is this cloth?	Yih kapṛā kitnā *lambā* hai?	Īn jāma chi ḳadar *darāz* ast?	Dā khamtā ṭsomra *plana* dah?
103 Put on your sheepskin coat.	Apnā postīn pahano.	Postīnat biposh.	Khpul postīn wāghunda.
104 They are *lazy* and negligent.	We *sust* aur ghāfil hain.	Ānān *kāhil* wa ghāfil hastand.	Haghoī *sust* au ghāfil dī.
105 You must go with me.	Tumko hamāre sāth jānā hogā.	Mī bāyad ki hamrāh i mā birawed.	Dzamā sara stā tlul boya.
106 What are you laughing at?	Kis sabab se hanste ho?	Chirā mī khanded?	Wale khānde?
107 *To laugh* without reason, is *foolish* (ness).	Be sabab *hansnā be wuḳūfī* hai.	Be sabab *khandīdan jihālat* ast.	Be sabab *khanda kam 'aḳlī* dah.
108 Come *with* me, I will go with you.	Hamare *sāth* āo, ham tumhāre sāth jāenge.	*Hamrāh* i man biyā, *bā* shuma khwāham raft.	Rā *sara* rāza, zuh ba dar *sara* zam.

English.	Urdū.	Persian.	Pashtū.
109 Remember this; do not forget to tell him.	Yād rakho, us se kahnā na bhūl jāo.	Yād dār ki guftan ba o farāmosh na kuned.	Yād lara chi haghuh ta dā wayal, her no ke.
110 When you *catch* a thief *punish* him severely, as a warning to *others*.	Jab tum chor *pakaṛo* to usko sakht *sazā do* ki *aur logoṅ* ko 'ibrat ho.	Wakte ki duzde *bigīred sazā* e sakht *bi dihedash* tā barāe *dīgarān* 'ibrat bāshad.	Kūm wakht chi ghal wunīse sakhtā *saza warka* chi *noro la* 'ibrat wī.
111 If you do not obey *orders you will be fined*.	Agar tum *ḥukm* na mānoge to *tum par jarīmāna hogā*.	Agar *ḥukm* bajā niyāred *jarīmāna karda khwāhed shud*.	Ka ta *ḥukum* wu na mane *jarīmāna ba she*.
112 That lady's children will play with their toys in the garden.	Us mem ṣāhib ke bābā log apne khilonoṅ se baghīche meṅ kheleṅge.	Aṭfāl i ān bībī ba bāzīchahāe (la'bati) khud dar bāghcha bāzī khwāhand kard.	Da haghe bībī halakān ba pa bāghcha ke da khpalo gudaio sara lobe kawī.
113 Shake the mosquito curtains and sweep the carpet.	Masahrī ko hilāo aur farsh ko jhāṛo.	Palangposh rā biyafshān wa farsh rā burob.	Da kaṭ parda wutsanda au farsh jāṛū ka.
114 It is my intention to go out *bear-shooting* the day after to-morrow.	Hamārā irāda hai kī parsoṅ *bhālū ke shikār* khelne ko jāweṅ.	Irāda darem ki pas i farda ba *shikār i khirs* rawem.	Dza mūng nyat dai chibul ṣabā *da melu kkhkār* ta lāṛ shū.

SECTION III.—ORDERS TO COOK AND TABLE-SERVANT.

English	Urdū	Persian	Pashtū
1 Get *breakfast* ready.	*Hāẓirī* taiyār karo.	*Nān i chāsht* taiyār kun.	*Nāshta* taiyāra ka.
2 Bring *dinner;* order the dinner.	*Khānā* lāo; khāne ke wāsṭe ḥukm do.	*Mez* taiyār kun; barāe taiyār kardan i nān ḥukm bidih.	*Ḍoḍai* rāwṛa; da ḍoḍai taiyarawulo da pāra ḥukm warkaṛa.

English.	Urdū.	Persian.	Pashtū.
3 Is the *dinner* ready?	*Khānā* taiyār hai?	*Nōn* taiyāṛ ast?	*Dodai* taiyāra dah?
4 Make the *tea*.	*Chā* banāo.	*Chāe* taiyār kun.	*Chāe* taiyāre ka.
5 Order them to make the *soup* hot.	Ḥukm do ki *sharūr* garm kareṅ.	Barāe garm kardan i *shorba* ḥukm bidih.	Warta wuwāya chi *shorwa* garma ka.
6 *Boil* some eggs.	Thoṛe aṇḍe *josh* (*bail*) *karo*.	Chand tā tu<u>kh</u>m *josh kun*.	Tso oye wu *ī<u>kh</u>awa*.
7 These eggs are not *fresh*.	Ye ande *tāze* nahiṅ.	Īn baiẓahā *tāza* nestand.	De oye *tāza* na dī.
8 Does the *water* boil?	*Pānī* khaultā hai?	*Ab* bajosh ast?	*Obuh* ī<u>kh</u>egī?
9 Bring a *cup and saucer*.	Ek *pirich piyāla* lāo.	Yak *na'lbakī* wa *piyāla* biyār.	Yuwa *piyāla* au *rakābaī* rāwṛā.
10 Bring a *dish*.	Ek *rikābī* lāo.	Yak *ḳāb* biyār.	Yau *tālai* rāwṛa.
11 Give me some *coffee* and sugar.	Thoṛā *kāfī* aur miṣrī hamko do.	*Ḳahwa* o ḳand mārā bidih.	Mā la laga *ḳahwa* au nabāt rāka.
12 Bring some *cream* or milk.	Kuchh *malāī* yā dūdḥ lāo.	Kadare *ḳaimāgh* yā shīr biyār.	Tsa lag *perawai* yā shande rāwṛa.
13 I will give you some tea and *lemon juice*.	Ham tumko kuchh chā aur *nimbū kā araḳ* deṅge.	Mā shumārā chīze chāe wa *'araḳ i līmūn* (*līmūnā*) <u>kh</u>wāhem dād.	Zuh ba tā ta laga chai au *da nimbū araḳ* darkam.
14 Some *butter* and jam are required.	*Makhan* aur murabbā chāhiye.	*Maska* o murabbā mī <u>kh</u>wāham.	Tsa lag kuch au murabbā pakār dī.
15 Bring a clean *spoon* and *stir* the sherbet.	Ṣāf *chamcha* lākar sharbat ko *hilāo*.	*Chamcha* i sāf āwurda sharbat rā *bujumbān*.	Pāka *tsamtsa* rāwṛa au pa sharbat ke ye *wuwaha*.
16 Put some *almonds* and raisins in the pulāo.	Palāo men *bādām* aur munaḳḳa dālo.	Dar palāo *bādām* o munaḳḳa biyandāz.	Pa pulāo ke tsa *bādām* au mawīz wāchawa.
17 There is a roast *lamb* and some *fish*.	*Halwān* kā kabāb aur *machhlī* haiṅ.	Kabāb i *barra* wa *māhī* ast.	Da *psuh* kabāb au *kab* dai.

English.	Urdū.	Persian.	Pashtū.
18 Take away the pistachio-nuts and bring *oranges*, quinces and preserved *pears*.	Pista lejāo, aur *nārangī*, bihī aur *nāshpātī* kā murabbā lāo.	Pista bi bar wa *nāranj*, bihī wa murabbā e *nāshpātī* biyār.	Pista yosa, au *naranjān*, bihai au da *naspatu* murabba rāwṛa.
19 Bring some *cool* water.	*Thanḍā* pānī lāo.	Āb i *khunak* biyār.	*Saṛe* obuh rāwṛa.
20 I like sugar candy, grapes and *figs*.	Miṣrī, angūr aur *anjīr* ko main pasand kartā huṅ.	Man bisyār shauḳ i ḳand, tāk o *anjīr* mī dāram.	Dzamā, nabāt, angūr, au *īnzir* khwakh dī.
21 This *pomegranate* is sour and the water-melon is *sweet*.	Yih *anār* khāṭṭā hai aur wuh tarbūz *mīthā* hai.	Īn *anār* tursh ast wa ān tarbūz *shīrīn* ast.	Dā *anār* trīw dai au endwanrah *khwagā* da.
22 The rind is *bitter;* do not swallow the stone.	Chilkā *kaṛwā* hai, guthlī mat niglo.	Postash *talkh* ast, tukhm ash rā az ḥalḳ faro mabar.	Postakai *trīkh* dai, da haghuh haḍūkai ma khura.
23 This meat is not well cooked, and is nearly all *bone*.	Yih gosht khūb pakkā nahīṅ, aur bahut *haddiyāṅ* haiṅ.	Īn gosht khūb pukhta nest, wa *ustukhwānhā* bisyār dārad.	Dā ghwakha khah pakha na dah au pa ke *hadūkī* ḍer dī.
24 The *cheese* is good, but the *sweetmeats* are stale.	*Panīr* achchhā hai, magar *mithāī* bāsī hai.	*Pānīr* khūb ast, magar *shīrīnī* bisyāṛ roza ast (tāza nest).	*Panīr* khuh dai, wale *khwāga* begānī dī.
25 He has eaten enough.	Usne peṭ bhar khāyā.	O pur shikam khurda ast.	Hagha pa khwāṛo kheṭa ḍaka kaṛī dah.
26 Cut the meat into small *pieces*.	Gosht ke chhoṭe chhoṭe *ṭukṛe* karo.	Gosht rā khurd khurd *pāra* kun.	Ghwakha waṛe waṛe tarāze ka.
27 Mix all sorts of *vegetables* together.	Sab ḳism kī *tarkārī* milāo.	Hama ḳism i *sabzīhā* biyāmez.	Ṭol rang *sābah* sara gaḍ ka.
28 *Pound* the spice well.	Maṣālaḥ khūb *pīso*.	Maṣālaḥ rā khūb *sāīdan bāyad*.	Maṣālaḥ khah *maida ka*.
29 *Pour* the wine into the water.	Sharāb pānī meṅ *ḍālo*.	Sharāb darāb *biyandāz*.	Sharāb pa obā ke *toī ka*.
30 The *apples* are not ripe, they should be red instead of *green*.	*Seb* pakke nahīṅ, bajāe *sabz* surkh chāhiye.	*Seb* pukhta nestand *sabz* hastand, bāyād ki surkh bāshand.	*Maṅṛe* pakhe na dī, boya chi sre wī na shue.

	English.	*Urdū.*	*Persian.*	*Pashtū.*
31	The mutton is very *fat.*	Maṭan (bherī kā gosht) bahut *charb* hai.	Gosht i gospand bisyār *charb* ast.	Da psa ghwakha ḍera *tsarba* da.
32	I am very hungry, bring whatever is ready.	Ham bahut bhūkhe haiṅ, jo kuchh taiyār hai lāo.	Man bisyār gurisna hastam har tu'ām ki taiyār bāshad biyār.	Zah ḍer wugai yam, har tse chi taiyār dī rāwṛa.
33	We shall want dinner as soon as we return.	Jab ham wāpas aweṅ use waḳt khānā chāhiye.	Waḳte ki wāpas āyem nān khwāhem khurd.	Kūm wakht chi mung rā wugarzū ḍoḍai ba ghwāṛū.
34	Mind you have breakfast ready punctually at nine *o'clock.*	Khabardār ki thīk nau *baje* hāẓirī taiyār howe.	Khabar dār ki ba nuh *baja* (*sā'at*) nān i chāsht taiyār bāshad.	Baidār osa chi nāshta pa no *bajo* taiyāra wī.
35	Tell the *villager* to milk the cow.	*Gāṅw wāle* se kaho ki gāo se dūdh dohe.	*Dihḳān* rā bugo ki az gāo shīr bi doshad.	*Kilīwāl ta* wuwāya chi da ghwa pai wu lweshī.
36	Kill two *fowls* and hang them up *till* to-morrow.	Do *murghī* ḥalāl karkar kal *tak* tāng rakho.	Do *mākiyān* ḥalāl karda *tā* fardā biyāwezānd.	Dwa *chirgān* ḥalāl ka au tar sabā pore ye zwaṛand kegda.
37	Pluck the fowl and skin the *kid.*	Murghī ke ṣirf par ukhāro aur *bakrī ke bachche* kī khāl utāro.	Mākiyān rā par bikash o *buz ghāla* rā post.	Da chirg wazar wu shūkawa au da *wuzḳūṛī* postakai wabāsa.
38	Roast the *partridge* on the spit.	*Tītar* ko sīkh par kabāb karo.	*Durrāj* rā ba sīkh kabāb kun.	*Tsenzarai* pa sīkh wupiya au wrīt ye ka.
39	Make a *charcoal* or a wood fire; do not use *cow-dung.*	*Koelā* yā lakṛī jalāo; *uplā* mat jalāo.	*Zughāl* yā chob bisozān, *sirgīn* masozān.	*Skāra* yā largī bal ka, *ghushāyuh* maseza.
40	That wood is *damp* and *will* not *burn.*	Wuh lakṛī *gīlī* hai, nahīṅ *jalegī.*	Ān hezam *tar* ast wa na *mī sozad.*	Hagha largai *lūnd* dai bal·ba na shī.
41	Tell the baker to bake some small loaves and bring some pickles and salt.	Rotī wāle se kaho ki kuchh chhoṭī rotī pakāwe aur tum kuchh achār aur namak lāo.	Nānpaz rā bugo ki chand tā nān i khurd bipazad wa shumā ḳadare achār wa namak biyāred.	Nānwāī (ḍoḍai pakhawunkaī) ta wuwāya chi waṛe ware ḍoḍaī pakhe ka au tā tsa achār au mālga rāwṛa.

English.	Urdū.	Persian.	Pashtū.
42 This bread is unleavened; put some yeast in the dough, and make leavened bread.	Yih roṭī paṭīrī hai; āte meṅ kuchh khamīr ḍāl kar khamīrī pakāo.	In nān faṭīrī ast; ḳadare khamīr dar ārd andākhta khamīrī pukhta kun.	Dā ḍoḍai patīrā dah; tsa lag khamīr pa oro ke gad ka au khamīrī pakha ka.

SECTION IV.—SEASONS AND WEATHER.

English.	Urdū.	Persian.	Pashtū.
1 In Peshawur the hot weather lasts for only three or four months.	Peshāwar meṅ ṣirf tīn chār mahīne garmī hotī hai.	Dar Peshāwar garmī ṣirf si chahār māh mī bāshad.	Pa Pekhāwar ke oṛai ṣirp dre tsalor myāshte wē.
2 The *cold weather* lasts for five or six months.	*Jāṛā* pānch chha mahīne hotā hai.	*Sarma* panj shash māh mī mānad.	*Zhamai* pīnza shpag mvāshte wī.
3 The sun is not hot in the winter, *even* in the middle of the day.	Jāṛe ke mausim meṅ do pahar ko *bhī* dhūp tez nahīṅ hotī.	Ba mausim i sarma ba nīm roz *ham* tāb i āftāb tez na mī bāshad.	Pa zhamī ke nmar pa takaṅṛa gharma *ham* garm na wī.
4 It is very cold in Cherāt, and it snows *frequently*.	Cherāt men bahut jāṛā hai aur *akṣar* barf paṛta hai.	Dar Cherāt bisyār khunakī ast wa *akṣar* barf mī uftad.	Pa Cherāt ke ḍer sāṛah dai, au akṣar *wāwra* waregī.
5 In that *district* the springs *are frozen* for two months.	Us *'ilāḳe* meṅ do mahīne tak chashma kā pānī *sardī se jam jātā hai*.	Ba ān *'ilāḳa* tā do māh chashmahā *yakh basta mī shawand*.	Pa hagha *'ilāḳa* ke chīne dwe myāshte *kangal kegī*.
6 When will the winter set in at Ghaznee?	Ghaznī meṅ jāṛā kab shurū' hogā?	Ba ghaznī sarma kai shurū' khwahad shud.	Pa ghaznī ke zhamai kila shurū kegī.

English.	*Urdū.*	*Persian.*	*Pashtū.*
7 Can we cross the *Pass before* the snow falls?	Barf paṛne se *pahle* is pahāṛ ke *kho* meṅ se ham jā sakte haiṅ?	*Pesh* az bārīdan i barf ba *darra* i īn koh raftan mī tawanem?	Da wāwre waredu na wṛānde mūng pa hagha *dara* ke ba ter shū?
8 What clothing is necessary in the cold weather?	Jāṛe men ẓarūrat kin kapṛoṅkī hotī hai?	Ba sarma kudām poshāk ba kār ast?	Pa zhamī ke tsa rang zaṛūkī pakār dī.
9 How long does the *summer* last in Kābul?	Kābul meṅ *garmī* kitnī muddat hotī hai?	Ba Kābul chand muddat *garmī* mī mānad?	Pa Kābul ke *oṛaī* tsomra wī?
10 The sky is *quite* clear.	Āsmān *khūb* ṣāf hai.	Āsmān *bi-l-kull* ṣāf ast.	Āsman *tak* shīn dai.
11 It is warmer to-day than *yesterday*, but *hail* fell the day before yesterday.	Āj garmī *kal* se ziyāda hai leken parsoṅ *olā* paṛā thā.	Imroz az *dīroz* garmī ziyāda ast magar parī roz *zhālā* bāī da būd.	Nan la *parūn* na garmī zyāta dah, wale bulparūn *zhalaē* waredatī wah.
12 It rained for three days without stopping.	Tīn din tak barābar pānī barastā rahā.	Tā si roz barābar bārān shud.	Dre wraze bula pase bārān wu shū.
13 The *harvest* will be ready in a month.	Ek mahīne ba'd *faṣl* taiyār hogā.	Pas az yak māh *faṣl* taiyār khwāhad shud.	Pa ywah myāsht ke *faṣal* ba taiyār wī.
14 It is very *cloudy*, I think it will rain soon.	*Bādal* bahut haiṅ hamārī dānist meṅ jald meṅh barsegā.	*Abr* bisyār ast yakīn ast ki bārān zūd khwāhad shud.	Dera *wryaz* dah gumān kawam chi bārān ba wu waregī.
15 If it is a fine day *saddle* my horse at *noon*.	Agar din ṣāf hai to *do pahar* ko hamāre ghoṛe par *zīn bāndho*.	Agar gard o ghubār na bāshad ba *nīm roz* asp i marā *zīn kun*.	Ka āsmān shīn wī no dzama ās pa *gharma zīn ka*.
16 Do not sleep out of doors, there is a heavy *dew* at night.	Bāhar mat so, rāt ko *os* bahut paṛtā hai.	Berūn khwāb na kuned *shab nam* bisyār mī uftad.	Bāhar ma tsamala dzaka chi dere *parkha* (*wāwre*) waregī.

English.	Urdū.	Persian.	Pashtū.
17 The trees will *blossom* in the spring and the *fruit* will be ripe in the *autumn*.	Bahār ke mausim meṅ darakht *phūleṅge* aur *sāonī* meṅ pakeṅge.	Ba mausim i bahār darakhthā *shigūfa mī kunand* wa ba mausim i *kharīf mewahā e* ānhā pukhta m̃ī shawand.	Pa sparlī ke ba wune wu tūkegī au pa *manī* ke ba *mewe* pakhe shī.
18 The climate of Kābul is very good.	Kābul kī āb o hawā bahut achchhī haiṅ.	Āb o hawā e Kābul bisyār khūb ast.	Da Kābul hawā derah khah dah.
19 The hot winds *blow* all day at Nowshera.	Naushahra meṅ tamām din lū *chaltī* hai.	Ba Naushahra tamām roz bād i samūm *mī wazad*.	Pa Naukhār ke ṭolah wraz garm bād *chalegī*.
20 *It lightens* very much now, and it *is beginning* to thunder.	Ab *bijlī* bahut *chamaktī* hai aur garajne *lagā*.	Aknūn *barḳ* bisyar mī *darakhshad* o ra'd ham *shurū' shud*.	Derah *brekhna dah* au ṭandar *ghrambegī*.
21 There was a storm in the *Hills* the day before yesterday.	Parsoṅ *pahāṛ* men āndhī thī.	Parī roz ba *kohistān* ṭūfān būd.	Bal parūn pa *ghrūno* bānde sīlaī wuh.

SECTION V.—NUMBERS, TIME AND AGE.

1 If three *are subtracted* from seven, four *remain*.	Agar sāt meṅ se tīn *nikāle jāeṅ* to chār bāḳī *rahte haiṅ*.	Agar az haft sī *tafrīḳ karda shawad* chahār *mī mānad*.	Ka la owo na dre wubāse tsalor *pāte kegī*.
2 Subtract ten from thirteen, how many remain?	Tera meṅ se das nikālā to kyā baḳī rahā?	Agar az sezdah dah hī dūr kunand chi khwāhad mānd?	Ka la dyār laso na las lare ke tso patī kegī?
3 *Add* five and two together.	Pānch aur do ko *jama' karo*.	Panj wa do rā *jama' kun*.	Pīnza au dwa *jama' ka*.
4 Eight and nine make seventeen.	Āṭh aur nau milkar satrah hotā hai.	Hasht o nuh haftdah mī shawad.	Atuh au nah owulas kegī.

English.	*Urdū.*	*Persian.*	*Pashtū.*
5 What is *half* twelve?	Bāra ka *ādhā* kyā?	*Niṣf* i duwāzdah chīst?	Da dwo laso *nīm* 'adad tso dai.
6 The third of eighteen is six.	Athārah kī tihāī chha.	Ṣulṣ i hezhdah shash mī shawad.	Dreyama ḥiṣṣa atallaso shpag dah.
7 A *quarter* of a hundred is twenty-five.	Sau kī *chauthāī* pachīs hai.	*Chahārum ḥiṣṣa* i ṣad bīst o panj mī shawad.	Da salo *tsalorama* brakha pīnza wīsht dah.
8 *Divide* sixteen by two.	Solah ko do par *bāṅto*.	Shānzdah rā ba do *taḳsīm kun*.	Shpāṛas pa dwo *wuwesha*.
9 What time is it?	Kitne baje haiṅ?	Kudām waḳt ast? (chand baja ast?)	Kūm wakht dai?
10 He has slept for two *hours*.	Wuh do *ghanṭe* se sotā hai.	O az do *sā'at* khufta ast.	Dwe *ganṭe* shīwī dī chi hagha uduh dai.
11 He stayed a *week* in Herāt.	Wuh ek *hafta* Herāt meṅ rahā.	O yak *hafta* ba herāt mānd.	Hagha ywah *hafta* pa Herāt ke pāte shuh.
12 I can only wait a *minute*.	Maiṅ ṣirf ek *lamḥa* ṭhahr saktā hūṅ.	Man ṣirf tā yak *lamḥa* mī tawānam mānd.	Zuh sirp ywah *laḥẓa* daredai sham.
13 There are *twice* as many men in this town as there are in that one.	Is ḳaṣbe meṅ us ḳaṣbe se *do chand* ādmī haiṅ.	Ahl i īn ḳariya *do chaud* i ān kariya hast.	Pa de kilī ke la hagha kilī na *dwo chaud* saṛe dī.
14 There are four times as many cows as goats.	Gāī bakrīoṅ se chār chand haiṅ.	Gāwān chahār chaud i buzhā ha hastand.	Ghāwe la chelo na chār chand dī.
15 I have one rifle for *each* sentry.	Hamāre pās *har ek* pahrewāle ke wāsṭe ek bandūḳ hai.	Barāe *har yak* pahradār yak tufang dāram.	Da *har yau* paradār de para yau ṭopak laram.
16 How old are you?	Tumhārī 'umr kitnī hai?	Shumā chand sālā hasted?	Ta da tso kālo ye?

	English.	Urdū.	Persian.	Pashtū.
17	I am twenty-one and my brother is twenty-four.	Merī 'umr iḳḳīs baras kī aur mere bhāī kī chaubīs baras kī hai.	'Umr i man bīst o yak sāl ast, wa barādaram bīst o chahār sālā ast.	Zuh da yowīsht au wror me da tsalor wīshto kālo dai.
18	The horse is three *years* and six months old.	Yih ghoṛā tīn *baras* aur chha mahīne kā hai.	'Umr i īn asp si *sāl* o shash māh ast.	Dā ās da dre nīmo kālo dai.
19	That old man has lived forty years in the same *village*.	Wuh buḍhā chālīs baras ek *gāṅw* meṅ rahā hai.	Ān pīr mard chihal sāl ba yak *dih* mānda ast.	Hagha spīngīrai tar tsalwekht kālo pore pa ywuh *kilī* ke ose dalai dai.
20	It is sixteen miles from that *end* of Peshawur to Pubbee.	Peshāwar ke us *sirre* se Pabbī solah mail hai.	Az ān *sūe* Peshāwar tā ba Pabbī shānzdah mīl ast.	Da Pekhāwar da haghe *khwā* na tar Pabaī pore shpāṛas mīla dī.
21	That *child* is only one year and a half old.	*Wuh bachcha* ṣirf ḍeṛh baras kā hai.	Ān *ṭifl* yak o nīm sālā ast.	Hagha *halak* da yau nīm kāl dai.
22	He *arrived* in good time, he is *never* late.	Wuh waḳt sir *pahunchā*, wuh *kabhī* der *nahīṅ* kartā.	O bar waḳt *rasīd*, o *gāhe* tākhīr *na* mī kunad.	Hagha pa wakht *rāghai hechere* nā wakht *na* kawī.
23	This man *always* comes a long time *after* the work is finished.	Wuh shakhṣ *hamesha* kām tamām karne se bahut der *pīchhe* ātā hai.	O *hamēsha ba'd* az ikhtitām i kār der karda mī āyad.	Hagha saṛai da kār pūrah kedo na derah mudah wrusto rāzi.
24	When the *moon* rises he will go home.	Jab *chānd* nikalegā tab wuh ghar jāegā.	Waḳte kī *māh* ṭulū' kunad (*or* barāyad) o ba khāna khwāhad raft.	Kūm wakht chi *myāsht* ra wukhegī hagha ba kor ta lāṛ shī.
25	Strike the *gong exactly* at 12 o'clock.	*Thīk* bāra baje *ghanṭā* bajāo.	*'Ain* ba nīm roz *jaras* rā bizan. (N.B. *jaras*, a bell.)	*Barābar* pa dwo las bajo *ganṭa* ghagawa.

English.	Urdū.	Persian.	Pashtū.
26 There was a fog the day before yesterday, but I hope we shall see the eclipse of the sun the day after to-morrow.	Parsoṅ kuhāsā thā, lekin ummed hai ki parsoṅ sūraj gahan dekheṅge.	Parī roz bukhār būd, lekin ummed ast ki pas i fardā kusūf khwāhem dīd.	Parūn dūnd wa wale ummed dai chi bal sabā ba nmar tandar nīwalai wuwīnu.

SECTION VI.—MONEY, WEIGHTS AND MEASURES.

English.	Urdū.	Persian.	Pashtū.
1 There are sixteen rupees in a gold mohr.	Ek ashrafī solah rupaye kī hotī hai.	Yak ashrafī ba shānzdah rupīya mī shawad.	Ywah butkaī ra shpāṛas rūpo kegī.
2 In Hindustan twelve pies make one *anna*, and sixteen annas one rupee.	Hindūstān meṅ bārah pāī kā ek *ānā*, aur solah āne kā ek rupiyā hotā hai.	Ba Hindūstān duwāzdah pāī yak *ānā* wa shānzdah ānā yak rūpīya mī shawad.	Pa Hindūstān ke da ywe *āne* dwalas pāī au da shpaṛas āno ywah rūpaī kegī.
3 In Teherān thirty falūs make one ḳarān, and ten ḳarāns make one tuman.	Ṭuhrān meṅ tīs falūs kā ek ḳarān aur das ḳarān kā ek tuman hotā hai.	Ba ṭuhrān sī falūs yak ḳarān wa dah ḳarān yak tuman mī shawad.	Pa tahrān ke da dersh fulūs yau krān au da las krāno yau tuman kegī.
4 Six annas and eight pie make one ḳarān.	Chha ānā āṭh pāī kā ek ḳarān hotā hai.	Shash ānā wa hasht pāī yak ḳarān mī shawad.	Shpag āne ātu pāī yau krān kegī.
5 What is the *price* of this?	Is kā *dām* kyā hai?	*Ḳīmat* ash chand ast?	Da de tso *baya* dah?
6 What is the lowest price you will take?	Kam se kam kyā dām loge?	Kam az kam chi ḳīmat khwāhed girift?	Le lago na laga baya ba tso ākhle?
7 Why is *grain* so *dear* here, when it is *cheap* in Kohāt?	*Ghalla* is jage *mahingā* kyūn hai, Kohāt meṅ *sastā* hai?	Īnjā *ghalla* chirā *girān* ast ba Kohāt *arzān* ast?	Dalta *ghala* wale domra *grāna* dah pa Kohāt ke kho *arzāna* dah?

English.	Urdū.	Persian.	Pashtū.
8 Go to the grainseller's and get this rupee *changed*.	Banye ke pās jākar iṣ rupīye ko *ṭoṛā* lāo.	Pesh i baḳḳāl rafta īn rūpiya rā *k͟hurda* kun.	Hindū tā lāṛ sha au da rūpaī *rāmāta* ka.
9 Give the three coolies five annas each, and pay one anna for the oil I bought.	Tīnoṅ ḳuliyoṅ ko pānch pānch ānā do; aur jo tel ham ne mol liyā us ke wāsṭe ek ānā do.	Ān sih ḳuliyān rā panj ānā fī nafar bidih; wa yak ānā bābat i rog͟han ki mā giriftem bidih.	De dre wāṛo mazdūrāno ta pīnza pīnza āne warka, au ywah āna da telo baya warka chi mā ak͟hastī dī.
10 You want twice as much as the other man does for a *shawl* exactly like this.	Is *shāl* kī ḳīmat dūgunī dūsre admī se kahte ho aur *shāl* waisa hī hai.	Ḳīmat i īn *shāl* do chand az shak͟hṣ i dīgar mī goed wa *shāl* i o hamrak͟ht i īn ast.	Tā da de *shāl* baya da hag͟h bul saṛī la *shāla* dwa chanda wāye dā au hag͟ha dwāṛa yo rang dī.
11 How many seers are there in a maund?	Ek man meṅ kitne sīr hote haiṅ?	Ba yak man chand sīr mī shawad?	Pa ywuh man ke tso sera wī?
12 How many pounds are there in a seer?	Ek sīr kaī paunḍ kā hotā hai?	Yak sīr chandpaun mī shawad.	Pa ywuh ser ke tso (paunḍ) nīm serī wī.
13 A Tabreez maund is five and a half pounds.	Ek man Tabrezī saṛhe pānch pāunḍ kā hotā hai.	Yak man i tabrezī az panj o nīm paun mī shawad.	Tabrezai man de pīnznīmo paunḍo kegī.
14 A *camel*-load is *generally* five maunds.	*Ūnṭ* kā bojh *akṣar* pānch man hotā hai.	Bār i *shutur akṣar* panj man mī shawad.	Da *ūk͟h* bār *akṣar* pīnzo manez wē.
15 Get a seer and a half of *rice* and three quarters of a seer of *ghee*.	Deṛh sīr *chāṅwal* aur tīn pāo *ghī* lāo.	Yak o nīm sīr *birinj* wa sih pāo *raug͟han i zard* biyār.	Yau nīm ser *wrizhe* au dre pāwa *g͟hweṛī* rāwṛa.
16 Give the horse a seer and three quarters of *barley*.	Ghoṛe ko paune do sīr *jau* do.	Asprā yak sīr o sih pāo *jau* bidih.	As la pāo kam dwa sera *orbushe* warka.
17 How much does this *copper* weigh?	Is *tāṅbe* kā wazan kitnā hai?	Wazan i īn *mis* chi ḳadar ast?	Dā *mis* tsomra drānuh dī?

English.	Urdū.	Persian.	Pashtū.
18 That *brass* weighs 13 tabreez maunds.	Yih *pītal* tera man tabrezī hai.	Īn *biranj* sezdah man i tabrezī ast.	Dā *zyar* pa tabrezī mnuh sara dyārlas mana dī.
19 Ask the *banker* for a *cheque* for 250 rupees on Peshāwar.	*Mahājan* se aṛhāī sau rupaye kī *hundwī* Peshāwar ke wāsṭe kaho.	Ba *sahūkār* bigo ki o do nīm sad rupīya rā *kaghaz i zar* ba Peshāwar bidihad.	*Ṣarrāf* ta wuwāya chi da dwa nīm sawo rupo *hundaī* pa Pekhāwar darkrī.
20 Bring the *scales* to weigh the silver.	Chāndī tolne ko *kānṭā* lāo.	Barāe wazan kardan (sanjīdan) i sīm *tarāzū* biyār.	Da spīn zaro talalo da pāra *tula* rāwṛa.
21 This is Delhi gold; it is not quite pure gold.	Yih Dihlī kā sonā hai; khāliṣ sonā nahīn.	Īn ṭilā e Dihlī ast; khāliṣ nest.	Dā da Dilī sruh zarr dī; kara na dī.
22 If he does not pay the *loan* his *creditor* will seize him.	Agar wuh *ḳarẓ* adā ne kare to *ḳarẓ khwāh* usko pakaṛegā.	Agar o *ḳarẓ* i khūd adā na kunad *ḳarẓkhwāh* o rā khwāhadgirift.	Ka hagha khpal *por* na adā kawī *porawuṛai* ba ye wunisī.
23 He will take his *debtor's* goods and his slaves.	Wuh apne *ḳarẓdār* ke asbāb aur ghulām lelegā.	O asbāb o ghulāmān i madyūn i khūd khwāhad girift.	Hagha ba da khpal *porawuṛī* māl asbāb au ghulāmān pa por ke trewākhlī.
24 You must pay the *principal* as well as the *interest*.	Tumko *aṣl* aur *sūd* dene chāhiye.	Bāyad ki shumā *aṣl* o *sūd* bidihed.	Tā 'la boya chi *aṣl* au *sūd* dwāṛa adā ke.
25 *Will you lend* me a hundred rupees for one month?	Tum hamko ek sau rupaye ek mahine ke wasṭe *ḳarẓ deoge*?	Shumā yak ṣad rupiya barāe yak māh *ba ṭaur i ḳarẓ* mārā *dādan mī tawāned*?	Da ywe myāshte pa neṭa ba tuh mā la sul rūpaī por rāke?
26 *Fill* the measure, but do not heap it up.	Paimāna barābar *bharo* ūnchā mat bharo.	Paimāna rā barābar *pur kun* ziyāda miyandāz.	O gai *ḍak ka* wale pre zyātawah ma.

English.	Urdū.	Persian.	Pashtū.
27 Make up your account to the end of last month, and I will pay you what is due in cash.	Apne ḥissāb ko guzre mahīne ke ākhir tak jama' karo aur jo kuchh bāḳī hai ham tum ko naḳd denge.	Ḥissāb i khud rā tā ākhir i māh i guzashta jama' kun wa har chi bāḳī ast naḳd khwāham dād.	Khpal ḥissāb da tere shewī miyāshte tar ākhir pore jama' ka au har tsa chi bāḳī wī rok ba darkam.
28 Is this kind of money current in Kābul?	Is ḳism kā sikka Kābul meṅ chaltā hai?	Dar Kābul inchunīn ẓarb rāij ast?	Pa Kābul ke dāse sikka chalegī?
29 Do not sell the jewels; give them in charge of my agent in Peshawur.	Jawāhir mat becho Peshāwar meṅ hamāre gumashte ko hawāle karo.	Jawāhir rā ma farosh dar Peshawar ba gumāshta i man bisipār.	Marghalare ma khartsawa pa Pekhāwar ke ye za mā gumāshta lā warka.

SECTION VII.—BOOKS AND OFFICE WORK

1 I want to write a *letter*: bring paper, *pen*, and *ink*.	Maiṅ *khaṭṭ* likhnā chāhtā hūṅ; kāghaẓ, *ḳalam*, *siyāhī* lāo.	Kāghaz *ḳalam* o *dāwāt* biyāred man mī khwāham ki *khaṭṭe* binawisam.	Zuh yau *khaṭṭ* līkal ghwāṛam kāghaẓ *ḳalam* au *mashwāṅṛaī* rāwṛa.
2 Write very clearly, so that I can *read* it easily.	Bahut ṣāf likho ki ham achchhī ṭaraḥ *paṛh* saken.	Khūb jalī binawīsed ki man *khwāndan* mī tawānam.	Pa khuh shān sara wulīka chi zuh ye pa asāntiya sara lwustai sham.
3 Tie up those letters in *bundles*.	We chiṭhīyaṅ *baste* meṅ bāndho.	Ān khaṭṭūṭ rā dar *basta* band kun.	Hagha khaṭūna pa *buḳcha* ke wutaṛa.

English.	*Urdū.*	*Persian.*	*Pashtū.*
4 Can you *draw* plans ?	Tum naḳsha *banā* sakte ho ?	Shumā naḳsha *kashīdan* mī tawāned ?	Tuh naḳsha *līkalai* she ?
5 Tell me if I pronounce the words right.	Ham se kaho ki hamārā talaffuz̤ durust hai ki nahīṅ.	Bi goed ki talaffuz̤ i man ṣaḥīḥ ast yā na.	Rāta wāya chi talaffuz̤ me kha dai ka na.
6 If I pronounce any word at all badly stop me.	Agar ham koī lafz̤ ghalaṭ kahen to hamko mana' karo.	Agar man kudām lafz̤ rā ghalaṭ khwānam marā mana' kun.	Ka zuh kūm lafz̤ ghalaṭ lwalam mana' me ka.
7 Cut this pen *nicely*, and mix the ink carefully.	Is ḳalam ko *achchhī ṭaraḥ* banāo aur siyāhī achchhī ṭaraḥ hilāo.	Īn ḳalam rā *ba khūbī* bitarāshed wa siyāhī rā ba hoshyāri bijumbāned.	Ḳalam *khuh* joṛ ka au siyāhī khah gaḍa ka.
8 The second *volume* of that book has 500 *pages*.	Us kitāb ke dūsre *jild* meṅ pānch sau *ṣafḥe* haiṅ.	Dar *jild* i doyum i īn kitāb panj ṣad *ṣafḥa* hast.	Da de kitāb pa doyam *jild* ke pīnzuh sawa *pāṇṛī* dī.
9 Read the first *chapter*.	Pahlā *bāb* paṛho.	*Bāb* i awwal bikhwān.	Awwal *bāb* lwala.
10 The *messenger* has arrived.	*Ḳāṣid* pahunchā hai.	*Ḳāṣid* rasīda ast.	*Ḳāṣid* rā rasedalai dai.
11 You must pay the postage before you break the *seal*.	*Muhr* ke kholne se peshtar maḥṣūl dene chāhiye.	Pesh az bardāshtan i *muhr* maḥṣūl dādan ẓarūr ast.	Da *muhr* prānato na wṛānde maḥṣūl adā kawul boya.
12 In what page is that *word* found ?	Wuh *lafz̤* kis ṣafḥa meṅ milegā ?	Ān *lafz̤* dar kudām ṣafḥa yāfta khwāhad shud ?	Hagha *lafz̤* pa kūma ṣafḥa ke milyā kegī ?
13 That book *was printed* in Lucknow.	Wuh kitāb Lakhnau meṅ *chhapī*.	Ān kitāb dar Lakhnau *maṭbū' shud*.	Hagha kitāb pa Lakhnau ke *chāp shawai dai*.
14 There is a *picture* at the beginning of the second chapter.	Dūsre bāb ke shurū' men ek *taṣwīr* hai.	Ba ibtidā e bāb i doyam yak *taṣwīr* ast.	Da dwayam bāb pa shurū' ke yau *taṣwīr* dai.
15 There is an *index* to the proverbs.	Mis̤lon kī ek *fihrist* hai.	Fihrist i *mis̤ālahā* ast.	Da matalūno yo *fihrist* shta.

English.	Urdū.	Persian.	Pashtū.
16 Is that *history* written in prose, or poetry ?	Wuh *tārīkh* naṣr yā naẓm meṅ hai ?	Ān *tārīkh* manṣūr yā manẓūm ast.	Hagha *tārīkh* naṣar dai ka naẓam ?
17 He has had a good education: he learnt three languages and a considerable amount of mathematics at school.	Usne achchhī ta'līm pāī ; madrase meṅ tīn zabāneṅ aur bahutsā 'ilm i riyāẓī sīkhā.	O ta'līm i khūb yāfta ast ; dar madrasa si zabānahā wa khaile 'ilm i riyāẓī amokht.	Haghuh khuh tarbīyat mundalai ; pa madrasa ke dre zhibe au khuh 'ilm da riyāẓ zdah kar.
18 The printer of the newspaper is ignorant, he has no knowledge.	Akhbār kā chhāpne wālā nādān hai kuchh 'ilm nahīṅ rakhtā.	Mutbi' i akhbār nādān ast 'ilm na dārad.	Da akhbār chāp kawunkai be 'aḳl dai 'ilm na larī.

SECTION VIII.—TRAVELLING AND SHOOTING.

1 Go up to the *top* of the hill.	Pahār kī *chotī* par chaṛh jāo.	Ba *ḳulla* i koh farār rau.	Da ghra pa *tsūka* wukhega.
2 Walk forward to the *edge* of the river.	Āge baṛho *kināre* naddī tak.	Pesh barau tā *lab* i daryā.	Da sīnd *ghāṛe* pure saṅ negh za.
3 First mount, and then *dismount*.	Pahle sawār hojāo phir *utarna*.	Awwal sawār shau bāz *pāyān shau*.	Awwal swor sha bya *kūz sha*.
4 Which is the way ?	Rastā kahāṅ hai ?	Rāh kujā ast ?	Lār kūma dah ?
5 Where does this *road* go to ?	Yiḥ *rastā* kahāṅ jātā hai ?	Īn *rāh* ba kujā mī rawad ?	Dā *lār* chartā zī ?
6 Take hold of the stirrup and *pull* it.	Rikāb ko pakaṛo aur *khīncho*.	Rikāb bigīr wa *bikash*.	Rikāb wunīsa au *rā ye kāga*.

English.	Urdū.	Persian.	Pashtū.
7 Bring *bread*.	*Roṭī* lāo.	*Nān* biyār.	*Ḍoḍaī* rāwṛa.
8 Bring grass, *corn* and water.	Ghās *dāna* aur pānī lāo.	Kāh *dāna* wa āb biyār.	Wākhuh *dāna* au obuh rāwṛa.
9 Sell me some milk and a lamb.	Dūdh aur ek bheṛī kā bachcha hamāre hāth becho.	Shīr o yak barra badast i man bafarosh.	Tsuh paī au yau psuh rābānde kharts ka.
10 Take the horse into the shade.	Ghoṛe ko sāye meṅ lejāo.	Asp rā ba sāya babar.	Ās sore ta boza.
11 Wake up the groom.	Sāīs ko jagāo.	Nafar rā bedār kun.	Sāīs baidār ka.
12 Who lives in that house?	Us ghar meṅ kaun rahtā hai?	Dar ān khāna ki mī mānad?	Pa hagh kor ke tsok osī?
13 The *temple* is near the village.	*Mandir* gāṅw ke nazdīk hai.	*But kada* mutaṣṣil i dih ast.	*Darmsāl* da kalī tsanga dai.
14 The villagers will go to the fields.	Gāṅw wāle kheṭ ko jāeṅge.	Dihḳānān ba kisht khwāhand raft.	Da kalī ālam ba paṭo ta zī.
15 Who is coming from the city?	Shahr se kaun ātā hai?	Az shahr ki mī āyad?	La khahar na tsok rādzī?
16 Shall I sleep in a house, or in my own *tent?*	Maiṅ kisī makān meṅ soūṅ yā apne *ḍere* meṅ?	Man dar khānae bikhuspam yā ba *khaima* i khud?	Za pa ywah kor ke tsamlam ka pa khpale *khima* ke?
17 Walk the horse about.	Ghoṛe ko tahlāo.	Asp rā kāwa kun (*or*, asp rā bigardān).	Ās wugarzawa.
18 *Pitch* the tent under those trees.	Un peṛoṅ ke nīche ḍera *khaṛā karo*.	Khīma rā zer i ān darakhthā *istāda kun*.	Pa hagho wuno lānde khīma *wudarawa*.
19 The *pole* is not upright.	*Chob* sīḍhā nahīṅ.	*Chob* rāst nest.	*Lakaṛa* negha na dah.
20 Pull the ropes tight.	Janāben khīṅcho.	Tanābhā bikash.	Paṛī rākāga.
21 Make some pegs.	Kuchh khūntīāṅ banāo.	Chand tā mekh taiyār kun.	Tsuh mogī joṛ ka.
22 Strike them with the *mallet*, and strike them hard.	*Mallaṭ* se thoṅko aur zor se thoṅko.	Ba *mekhkob* bikobash wa ba zor bizan.	Pa ḍabalī sara ye waha au maẓbūṭ ye khakh ka.
23 Pack up the tents, put them in the bags, and load the camels with them.	Deroṅ ko lapeṭ kar aur shalī-toṅ meṅ band karkar unṭoṅ par lādo.	Khīmahā rā tah namūda wa miyān i shalīta band karda bar shuturān bār kun.	Hagha khime wunghāṛa au pa khalto ke ye wāchawa au pa ūkhāno ye bār ka.

English.	Urdū.	Persian.	Pashtū.
24 Pack up the *baggage* and place a *watchman* over it.	*Asbāb* band karkar ek *chokīdār* muḳarrar karo.	*Asbāb* rā band karda *chokīdār* bālāyash muḳarrar kun.	*Asbāb* wutaṛa au yo *tsaukidār* pse muḳarrar ka.
25 Is the *boat* ready?	*Kishtī* taiyār hai?	*Kishtī* taiyār ast?	*Beṛaī* taiyāra dah?
26 Can a horse walk into the boat, or must he *jump* in?	Ghorā kishtī men is ṭaraḥ se jā saktā hai yā *kūdkar* jāegā?	Asp īn ṭaur ba kishtī darāmadan mī tawānad yā *jast* kunad?	Āspa beṛai ke ase khatai shī ka *ṭop* ba wahī?
27 Go to the horse's head and *pat* him.	Ghoṛe ke sīr ke pās jā kar use *tapkī do.*	Nizd i asp rafta ba sarash *dast bimāl.*	Da ās sar ta lāṛ sha au lās pre wuwaha.
28 Speak to him, and do not *flurry* him.	Use chimkāro aur use mat *darāo.*	O rā āwāz dāda rām kun wa ma *tarsānash.*	Da mīne khabare warsara wuka *werawaye* mā.
29 If the horse *is frightened*, wait.	Agar ghoṛā *dare* to thahro.	Agar asp *mī tarsad* ṣabr kun.	Ka ās *wyaregī*, wudarega.
30 Lead him by a *loose* rein, and make him trot to the edge.	Lagām dhīlā pakaṛkar kināre tak dulkī lejāo.	Lagām *narm* girifta tā kināra ba poya bibar.	Ḳaizā *narma* wunīsa tar kināre pareye dulkī ka.
31 Lead all the horses over the bridge, and drive the *cattle* through the river.	Sab ghoṛe pul ke ūpar se lejāo, aur *dawāb* naddī meṅ se hānk kar lejāo.	Aspān rā ba pul bibar wa dīgar *haiwānāt* rā az pāyāb bibar.	Ṭol āsūna pa pūl pore ka, au *dangar* pa sīnd war nanabāsa chi tre pore shī.
32 The *girths* are not tight, tighten them; loosen the girths.	*Tang* kasā hūā nahīṅ usko khīncho; tang ḍhīlā karo.	*Tang* narm ast bikash ash; tang narm kun.	*Tang* maẓbūṭ na dai rāye kāga, tang sust ka.
33 Put on the *bridle*, and do not *leave go* of the horse till my foot is in the stirrup.	*Lagām* chaṛhāo, aur ghoṛe ko mat *chhoṛo* jab tak hamārā pāṅw rikāb men māẓbūṭ na ho.	*Ḳaiza* kun o asp rā ma *guzār* tā ān ki pāyam ba rikāb dar āyad.	*Ḳāiza* warpa sar ka au tar tso pore chi pkhe me rikābo ta khe rasedalī na dī ās ma pregda.

English.	Urdū.	Persian.	Pashtū.
34 Make the stirrups *both* alike, take them up one hole; let the other down two holes.	*Donoṅ* rikāb barābar karo, unko ek ghar (surākh) ūṅchā karo; dūsrī ko do ghar nīche karo.	*Har do* rikāb rā barābar kun yak khāna ānhā rā bālā kun; dīgar do khāna faro kun.	*Dwāṛa* rikā būna barābar ka yo sūṛai ye uchat ka; bul dwa sūrī kūz ka.
35 Can I get a horse at the village?	Is gāṅw meṅ hamko ghoṛā milegā?	Ba īn dih asp khwāham yāft?	Pa de kalī ke ba ās mūmam.
36 Will you let me have a pony *on hire?*	Hamko ek ṭaṭṭū *karāye par* doge?	Yak yābū mārā *ba karāya* khwahed dād?	Mā la ba yo tatū *pa kirāya* rāke?
37 Put the saddle, bridle and saddle-cloth in the tent.	Zīn, lagām aur zīnposh ḍere men rakho.	Zīn lagām o zīnposh darūn i khīma binih.	Zīn, ḳāiza, au zīnposh pa khīma ke kegda.
38 Cover them with a *blanket.*	Unpar ek *kamal* dālo.	Bālāyash *shālake* biyandāz.	Pa ywah shaṛaī ye puṭ ka.
39 Take off the bridle and put on a *halter.*	Lagām utāro aur *agāṛī* lagāo.	Ḳaiza rā bikash wa *kamand i pesh* bi band.	Ḳāiza tre kūza ka au tarsarai wur pa sar ka au wu ye taṛa.
40 Put on the head and heel ropes, and spread some *straw.*	Agāṛī pichhāṛī lagākar *bichhālī* bichhāo.	Rasanhā e pesh o pas basta zerash *kāh* bugustarān.	Agāṛai pichāṛai wulagawa au *lūkha* wughoṛawa.
41 Take care; keep the horses *apart.*	Khabardār ghoṛoṅ ko *alag* rakho.	Khabar dār aspān rā *alaḥda alaḥda* bi mān.	Khabardār osa chi āsūna *byal byal* wutaṛal shī.
42 Can the horses go round and meet me on the other *bank* of the river, or at the other *side* of the hill?	Ghoṛe ghūmkar jā sakte haiṅ ki ham ko us *kināre* daryā par yā us *ṭaraf* pahāṛ ki mileṅ?	Aspān ān sū gashta raftan mī tawānand ki mā ānhā rā ba ān *lab* i daryā yā ān *sūe* koh biyabem?	Āsūna tre chār chaper tlaī shī chi da daryāh pa hagha ghāṛa yā da ghruh pa hagha khwa rāta milya shī?
43 Is the horse *quiet* or vicious?	Yih ghoṛā *gharīb* yā badma'āsh hai?	Īn asp *gharīb* yā badma'āsh ast?	Hagha ās *aṣīl* dai ka kam aṣl?
44 Will the pony go in harness, or *does he kick?*	Yih ṭaṭṭū gāṛhī men jāegā yā *lāt mārtā?*	In yābū ba gāṛhī khwāhad raft yā *laghad mī zanad?*	Dā tatū pa gādai ke zī ka *late wahī.*

English.	Urdū.	Persian.	Pashtū.
45 I shall start early in the morning; an hour before *sunrise*.	Maiṅ sawere ek ghantā *sūraj nikalne* se pahle rawāna hūṅgā.	Man 'alā al ṣabāḥ yak sā'at pesh az *tulū 'i āftāb* rawāna khwābam shud.	Ṣabāī wakhte la nmar khato na ywah garai wṛānde ba zam.
46 We shall rest till the *afternoon*.	Ham *tīsre pahar* tak muḳām kareṅge.	Mā tā *sipahar* īnjā ḳaiyām khwāhem kard.	Mūng ba tar māspekhin pure pāte kegū.
47 In the *evening*, when it is cool, get ready for the *journey*.	*Shām* ke waḳt jab kuchh ṭhandh ho *safar* kī taiyārī karo.	Ba waḳt i *shām* ki khunak shawad sāmān i *safar bukuned*.	Mākhām chi sardī shī da *safar* taiyārī kuwaī.
48 Call three coolies, and *distribute* the *loads* equally.	Tīn ḳulī bulākar barābar *bojh banṭ do*.	Si ḳulī talbīda *bārhā* rā barābar *taḳsīm kun*.	Dre muzdūrān rāwala au ṭolo tah barābar barābar *bār warkṛa*.
49 The horse has dropped a shoe; call a *farrier* at once.	Ek na'l ghoṛe kā na'l gīr gayā, *na'l band* ko jhaṭ paṭ bulāo.	Yak na'l i asp uftāda *na'l band* rā zūd bi ṭalbān.	Da ās yo na'l prewut *na'l band* dastī rāwulola.
50 Put on the old shoe again.	Purānā na'l phir bāndho.	Na'l i kuhna bichaspān.	Zoṛ na'l baya wulagawa.
51 Make a new shoe.	Ek nayā na'l banāo.	Yak na'l i nau bi sāz.	Yo nawai na'l joṛ ka.
52 Do not cut the *frog*, *fit* the shoe carefully.	*Putlī* mat kāṭo, na'l *khabardārī se biṭha* o.	Miyān i sum ma bur *na'l* ba *hoshyārī binishān*.	Da sūm talai ma prekawah na'l pa hokhyārai sara wulagawa.
53 Take care that the edge of the shoe does not catch the other foot.	Khabardār ki na'l kā kināra durust ho ki jis se newar ne laje.	Hosh kun ki sar i na'l barābar bāshad ki asp par na zanud.	Khabar dār chi na'l da ywe pkhe pa bula pkhe na lagī.
54 The shoe of the *hind foot* is too long, and catches the *fore* foot.	*Pichhlī pāṅw* kā na'l bahut baṛā hai wuh *agle* pair ke na'l men lagtā hai.	Na'l i *pāe pasīn* i asp darāz ast *pāe peshīn* rā mī zanad.	*Dạ wrustanai pkhe* na'l der ūgd dai au wṛandīnai pkha nasī.

English.	Urdū.	Persian.	Pashtū.
55 *File* off the edge.	Uskā sirra *ret do.*	Sar ash rā *sūhān kun.*	Kināra ye *sohān ka.*
56 Mind you arrive in camp in time, make no *delay.*	Khabardār, paṛāo meṅ bar waḳt pahuncho, *der* na ho.	Khabardār ba manzil bar waḳt biras, *tākhīr* ma kun.	Baidār sha chi manzil la pa wakht rāwurase, *dīl* ma kṛa.
57 Let there be no delay on the road, and keep all the camels together.	Raste meṅ der mat karo aur sab ūnt ikhatte lejāo.	Ba rāh tākhir ma kun wa hama shuturān rā yak jāe bibar.	Pa lār hets dīl ma kṛah au ūkhān tol jama' rāwala.
58 Borrow a *bedstead* from the village, and light a fire.	Ek *chārpāī* gāṅw se māng lo aur āg jalāo.	Yak *palang* az dih biṭalab wa ātish bisozān.	Yo *kaṭ* la kalī na ra wughwāṛa au or balka.
59 Tell them to bring clear drinking water and dry fire-wood.	Unko kaho ki ṣāf pānī pīne ke wasṭe aur sūkhī lakṛī jalāne kī lāweṅ.	Eshān rā bugo ki āb i ṣāf barāe noshīdan wa hezm i khushk biyārand.	War ta wu wāya chi pāke sāfe obuh tsko la au wuche largī swo la rāwṛī.
60 This ground is *soft*, *look for* a dry place.	Yih zamīn *narm* hai, ek sūkhī jagah *talāsh karo.*	In jā e *narm* ast, jāe khushk *talāsh* kun.	Dā zmoka *narma* dah cherta wuch zāi *wugora.*
61 My horse *died* yesterday, I wish to buy *another.*	Merā ghoṛa kal *mar gayā*, maiṅ chāhtā ki *dūsrā* mol lūṅ.	Aspam dīroz *murd*, mī khwā-ham ki *dīgar* bi kharam.	Ās me parūn maṛ shu zaka bul ās ākhestal ghwāṛam.
62 What is the price of the white *mare?*	Us sufed *ghoṛī* kī kyā ḳīmat hai?	Ḳīmat i ān *mādīyān* i sufed chīst?	Da haghe spine *aspe* baya tso dah?
63 What will you take for the *bay?* is he a *gelding?*	Us *kumed* ke wāsṭe kyā dām loge? wuh *akhta* hai?	Barāe ān *kumed* chi ḳīmat khwāhed girift? *akhta* ast?	Da sūr ās ba tso ḳīmat wākhle *akhta* (khasī) dai.
64 Tell the groom to *rub* the horse down well.	Sāīs se kaho ki ghoṛā achchhī ṭarah *male.*	Sāīs rā bugo ki asp rā khūb *mālish bukunad.*	Sāis ta wuwāya chi ās khah *wu mugī.*
65 Let two men rub the horse down, one on each side.	Do ādmī ghoṛe kī mālish kareṅ, ek ek donoṅ ṭaraf.	Yak yak har sū istāda do nafar asp rā bimāland.	Dwa saṛē da ās wu mugī yo yo khwa bul bul khwa.

English.	Urdū.	Persian.	Pashtū.
66 Water the horse in the morning, and give him *bran* and *grain* three times a day.	Ṣubḥ ko g͟hoṛe ko pānī pilāo ; aur tīnoṅ waḳt *chokar* aur *channā* k͟hilāo.	'Alā ul ṣabāh asp rā āb bidih wa har sih waḳt *sabūs* o *nāk͟hūd.*	Ṣabaī ās la obuh warka au pa wraz ke dre zulla *chokar* au *çhanre* warkawa.
67 Take the horse to the river and wash him.	Ghoṛe ko naddī meṅ lejākar nahlāo.	Asp rā ba daryā burda busho yash.	Ās sīnd ta boza au wu ye lambawa.
68 Are there any snipe in that marsh?	Us jbīl meṅ kuchh chāhe milte haiṅ?	Dar ān chaman murg͟hābī e k͟hurd yāfta mī shawand.	Pa hag͟ha jīl ke tsuh kakawī milye kegī?
69 Collect twenty villagers to beat for game.	Bīs gāṅwāle jama' karo ki shikār hāṅkeṅ.	Bist dihḳānān bi ṭalbān ki shikār rā bark͟hezānand.	Da kalī shul saṛī rāwubolā chi kk͟hkār purtaka.
70 Have you seen any duck flying over the river?	Tum ne kuchh baṭakeṅ naddī ke ūpar uṛtī dekhī haiṅ?	Shumā kudām baṭhā rā bar ān daryā parān dīda ed?	Tāso tsuh elaī pa sīnd bānde ālwa tunkā līdalī dī?
71 How soon will quail be found in this country?	Baṭere is mulk meṅ kitne dinoṅ meṅ mileṅge?	Dar īn mulk būdana ba'd az chand muddat yāfta k͟hwā-bad shud?	Pa de mulk ke ba maṛaze pa tso razo ke paidā shī?
72 Bring the other gun and keep close to me.	Dūsrī bandūḳ lākar hamāre nazdīk raho.	Bandūḳ i dīgar āwurda nizd i man bimān.	Bul tupak rāwṛa au dzamā pa tsang osā.
73 Get ten cartridges out of the bag and be ready to give them me.	Das kārtūs thailī meṅ se nikālkar hamko dene ke wasṭe taiyār rakho.	Dah kārtūs āz kīsa bar āwurda barāe dādan am taiyār dār.	Las kārtūsa la kīse na rā wu bāsa au rākawalo lā ye tai-yār lara.
74 I shall hide behind those reeds: drive all the game towards me.	Ham in sarkandoṅ ke pīchhe chhip raheṅge, sab shikār hamāre ṭaraf hāṅk lāo.	Mā pas i īn naiistān poshīda k͟hwāhem mānd tamām shi-kār rā ba sūe mā birān.	Zuh ba la de derwyo wrusto put sham, tol kk͟hkār rā bānde rāwala.
75 Beat the bushes well and make the birds rise.	Jhāṛiyoṅ ko k͟hūb mār kar pakherūoṅ ko uṛāo.	Botahā rā k͟hūb bi zan tā parin-dahā bark͟hezand.	Būtī k͟hūb wuwaha chi tre marg͟hān wālūzī.

English.	Urdū.	Persian.	Pashtū.
76 What are those birds flying over the hill, and those feeding in the field?	We chiriye jo pahār ke upar uṛte haiṅ kyā aur jo khet meṅ chugte haiṅ kyā haiṅ?	Ān parindagān ki bar kohistān mī parand kudām wa ān ki dar kishtahā mīcharand kudām ḳism and?	Hagha marghān chi pa ghruh ālūzī tsuh au hagha chi pa toke tsurī tsuh dī?

SECTION IX.—RECONNOITRING.

English.	Urdū.	Persian.	Pashtū.
1 Have you seen any men going in that *direction*?	Tum ne koī ādmī us *ṭaraf* jāte dekhe?	Shumā kudām mardumān ba ān *sū* rawān dīda ed?	Tā kūm saṛī hagh tsang ta tlūnkī wulīdal?
2 Were they walking or *riding?*	We piyāda jate the yā *sawār?*	Eshān piyāda mī raftand yā *sawār?*	Haghoī pyāda tlal ka *swāruh?*
3 Some were walking and one was in a (*sedan*) dooly.	Kaī ek piyāda jāte the aur ek *ḍolī* men.	Chand nafar piyāda mī raftand wa yak dar *pālkī* sawār bud.	Zine pyāda wū au yopa *pālkaī* ke wuh.
4 How many men were there?	Kitne ādmī the?	Chand kas būdand?	Tso saṛī wū?
5 They went over the hill, but returned and stood on the top.	We pahār ke ūpar se gae lekin phir laut kar chotī par khaṛe hūe.	Eshān az bālāe koh raftand lekin bāz āmāda ba sar i koh istāda shudand.	Haghoī da ghruh pa hagh tsang lāṛal, wale rawūgarze dal au pa ṣar ye wudare dal.
6 Were they *soldiers* or villagers?	We *sipāhī* the yā gāṅw wāle?	Eshān *sipāhī* būdand yā dih ḳānān?	Haghoī *spāyān* wū ka kalīwāl.
7 They were soldiers and *workmen*.	We sipāhī aur *mazdūr* the.	Sipāhī o *mazdūr* būdand.	Haghoī spāyān au mazdūrān wū.

English.	Urdū.	Persian.	Pashtū.
8 How long is it since they passed you?	Kitnī der hūī ki tumhāre pās se guzar gaye?	Chand der shuda ast ki ba shumā mulāḳī shuda guzashtand.	Tso mudda shawī dah chi haghoī pa tā ter shwul.
9 How long is it since they went out of sight?	Kitnī der hūī ki we sāmhne se chale gae?	Chand gāh ast ki az naẓar ghāib shudand?	Tso mudda shawī dah chi haghoi lāṛal?
10 They passed here one hour or one hour and a half ago.	Ek yā deṛh ghantā hūā ki we yahān se gae.	Yak yā yak o nīm sā'at shuda ki az īnjā rafta and.	Ywah yā ywah nīma ganṭa wu shwa chi haghoī dalta ter shwul.
11 Is that a city, a town or a village?	Wuh shahr yā ḳaṣba yā gāṅw hai?	Īn shahr yā ḳaṣba yā dih ast?	Hagha khahr dai ka kasba ka kalai?
12 What is *behind* that tree?	Us peṛ ke *pīchhe* kyā hai?	*Pas* i ān darakht chīst?	Da haghe wune na *wruste* tsa dī?
13 How far is it to Peshawur?	Yahān se Peshāwar kitna dūr hai?	Az īnjā Peshāwar chi ḳadar dūr ast?	Pekhāwar la de zāi na tsomra lare dai?
14 How long will it take to walk to the top of the hill?	Kitne 'arṣe meṅ pahāṛ ke ūpar pahuncheṅge?	Ba chand 'arṣa bālāe koh khwahem raft?	Pa tso mudda ba dā ghruh sar ta wu khegū.
15 Can a horse go through the water?	Ghoṛā is pānī meṅ se jā saktā hai?	Asp az īn āb 'ubūr kardan mī tawānad?	Ās la de obo na pore kedai shī?
16 Can a man walk *across* the river in the hot season?	Garmī men ādmī is naddi *se* pāyāb jā saktā hai?	Ba mausim i garma kase az īn rūd pāyāb *'ubūr* kardan mī tawānad?	Pa oṛī ke la de daryāb na saṛai *pore* kedai shī?
17 Are there boats here in the rains?	Barsāt meṅ yahāṅ kishtī hotī haiṅ?	Ba mausīm i bārish dar īn jā kishtī mī bāshad?	Pa bashakāl ke dalta beṛai wī?
18 Are there any trees in the ravine?	Is *nāle* meṅ koī peṛ hai?	Ba in *jū* darakhthā hastand?	Pa hagh *khwaṛ* ke tsa wune shta?

English.	Urdū.	Persian.	Pashtū.
19 Do the hill men bring wood from the *forest?*	Pahāṛī log lakṛī *jangal* se lāte haiṅ?	Mardumān i kohī hezm az *jangal* mī ārand?	Da ghruh khalḳ largī la *zangal* na rāwṛī?
20 Can a horse go across that ravine?	Ghoṛā us nāle ke pār ho saktā hai?	Asp az miyān i īn jū raftan mī tawānad?	Ās la hagh khwaṛ na pore kedai shī.
21 I do not want to go *fast*: can a horse walk there?	Ham *jald* nahīṅ jāne chāhte: ghoṛā wahāṅ ḳadam ḳadam chal saktā hai?	Mā *zūd* raftan na mī khwāhem: ānjā asp ḳadam ḳadam raftan mī tawānad?	Zah *pa dau* tluh na ghwāṛam: ās pa ḳadam ḳadam tlai shī?
22 Do the villagers' ponies go by that road?	Gāṅw wāloṅ ke ṭaṭṭū us raste jāte haiṅ?	Yābūhāe dihḳānān ba īn rāh mī rawand?	Da kalīwālo ṭaṭūgān pa dā lār tlaī shī.
23 Walk *in front* and see how much water there is.	*Āge* jākar dekho ki pānī kitnā hai?	*Pesh* rafta bibīn ki āb chi ḳadar ast.	*Wṛānde* lāṛ sha au wugora chi obuh tsomra dī.
24 Is the ground *stony*, or full of holes?	Zamīn *patthrelī* yā chhed chhed hai?	Zamīn *sangī* yā sūrākhdār ast?	Ā zmoka kāṅṛīza dah ka sūṛe larī?
25 Are the people here settled, or nomad?	Is jage ke log mudāmī mutawaṭṭin haiṅ ki chand roza?	Mardumān i īnjā mutawaṭṭinān i dāimī and yā khāna ba dosh?	Da de zai khalḳ hamesha osedunkī dī yā kochiyān dī?
26 Were they *armed?*	*Unke pās* koī *hathyār* the?	*Aslaḥ dār* būdand?	Haghoī *wasla dār* wū?
27 They had *most* of them *muskets* and scimetars: some had only *daggers*.	*Akṣāroṅ* ke pās *bandūḳ* aur talwār thī aur kaī ek ke pās ṣirf *chhure* the.	*Akṣar tufang* o shamsher dāshtand wa ba'ẓe ṣirf *peshḳabẓ*.	Da ḍero zakhá *ṭopak* au tūre we au da zeno zakha *chāṛe* we.
28 Who is the head man of that village? to what *tribe* does he belong?	Us gāṅw meṅ kaun lambardār haí, wuh kis *ḳaum* kā hai?	Ba ān dih nambar dār kīst, wa āz kudām *ḳabīla* ast?	Da hagh kalī maluk tsok dai au da kūm *ḳaum* dai.
29 Is there any man who speaks Persian here?	Yahān koī fārsī bolne wālā hai?	Īnjā kase farsī mī goyad?	Dalta dāse saṛai shta chi fārsī wāyī?

	English.	Urdū.	Persian.	Pashtū.
30	Find a man who knows Hindūstānī.	Talāsh karo kī koī Hindūstānī bolne wālā hāth loge.	Talāsh i kudām Hindī go kuned.	Yo saṛai wu laṭawa chi Hindko pohegī.
31	Speak very *slowly*.	Bahut *āhisti* bolo.	Bisyār *āhisti* bugo.	Ḍer *roro* wāya.
32	Speak very *distinctly*.	Bahut *ṣaḥīḥ* bole.	Bisyār *ṣaḥīḥ* bugo.	Ḍer *ṣaḥīḥ* wāya.
33	Use Persian words in place of Pashtu words as much as you can.	Jitnā mumkin hai bajāe alfāẓ Pashtū ke Fārsī ke lafẓ hoṅ.	Har ḳadar ki mumkin ast bajāe alfāẓ i Pashtū Farsī bugo.	Da Paḳhto pa zai tsomra chi darna ḳegī domra da Fārsī lafẓūna wāya.
34	Do you understand me? I do not understand you.	Tum hamārī bāt samajhte ho? Ham tumhārī bāt nahīṅ samajhte.	Shumā sukhanhā e mārā mī fahmed? man ḳalām i shumā na mi fahmam.	Dzmā pa khabaro pohege? zuh na pohegam.
35	*Translate* what he says into Persian.	Jo kuchh wuh kahe uskā *tarjuma* fārsī meṅ *karo*.	Har chi o mī goyad *tarjuma* ash ba zabān i farsī *bukun*.	Tso chi dai wāyī pa fārsī ye *kah*.
36	Tell him in Pashtu what I say in Hindūstānī.	Use Pashtū men kaho jo ham Hindustāni meṅ kahte haiṅ.	Ba o ba zabān i Pashtū bugo har chi man ba zabān i Hindī mī goyam.	Zah chi tsa pa hindko ke wāyam pa Pukhto ke warta wu wāya.
37	Send a man with me to show me the way.	Ek ādmī hamāre sath karo ki rasta dikhāe.	Yak shakhṣ hamrāh i man bifirist ki rāh bi numāyad.	Lār khayalo la rāsara yo saṛai wāstawa.
88	Which is the road to Peshāwar? which road is the shortest?	Peshāwar kā rastā kaunsā hai? kaunsā rastā nazdik hai?	Rāh i Peshāwar kudām ast? wa kudām rāh nazdiktar ast?	Da Pekhāwar lār kūma dah? kūma lār landa dah?
39	Is the road *metalled* or unmetalled? Is it good to *gallop* a horse on?	Rastā *pakkā* yā kachchā hai? ghoṛe ke *daurāne* ke wasṭe achchhā hai?	Rāh *pukhta* ast yā khām? barāe *duwānidan* i asp khūb ast?	*Pakha* lār dah ka kacha au da ās *zghaledo* la khah dah ka na?
40	How many watercourses are there in the way?	Is rāste men kitnī nāliāṅ haiṅ?	Ba īn rāh chand jū hast?	Pa lār ke tso lakhtī dī?

English.	Urdū.	Persian.	Pashtū.
41 Are the banks steep or *sloping*, and is the *bottom* soft ?	Kināre khaṛe haiṅ yā *salāmī* meṅ aur *bīch* meṅ narm hai ?	Aṭrāf istāda hastand yā *salāmī dār ?* wa *miyāna* ash gil i narm ast ?	Ghāṛe neghe dī ka *salāmī* au *manz ye* narm dai.
42 Is the bed of the river stony ?	Naddī kī zamīn pathrelī hai ?	Rūd khāna sangdār ast ?	Da daryāb tal kanṛīz dai ?
43 Is that slope steeper than this?	Wuh salāmī is se khaṛī hai ?	Ān salāmī az īn istādatar ast ?	Ā slāmī la de na negha dah ?
44 How many heads of families live in this village, and who is the *chief ?*	Is gāṅw meṅ kitne 'aiyāl dār haiṅ aur un meṅ kaun *sardār* hai ?	Dar īn dih chand 'aiyāl dār hastand wa *sardār* i ānhā kīst ?	Pa de kalī ke tso kade osī au tsok ye mashar *malak* dai?
45 There are two thousand five hundred inhabitants in that town.	Us ḳaṣbe men do hazār pānch sau ādmī haiṅ.	Ba ān ḳaṣba do hazār o panj sad kas hastand.	Pa hagha ḳaṣba ke dwa nīm zara osedūnkī dī.
46 Are the women and children *included* or not ?	Is meṅ zan o bachcha *shāmil* haiṅ yā nahīṅ ?	Dar īn shumār zan o bachcha *shāmil* ast ?	Pa ke khaze au halakān *shāmil* dī ka na ?
47 How many cattle have they ?	Unke pās kitne dawāb haiṅ ?	Chand māl i māweshī dārand ?	Haghoī tsomra māl larī ?
48 Is there a grain-seller, and how much grain and *flour* has he in store ?	Koī banyā hai aur uske pas kitnā dāna aur *ātā* hai ?	Kudām baḳḳāl ast wa chi ḳadar dāna wa *ārd* dārad ?	Tsok ghalla farosh shta ? au tsomra dāna au *oṛah* larī ?
49 What *supplies* can be obtained in this country ?	Is mulk meṅ kyā *rasad* milegā?	Ba īn mulk kudām *ajnās* ḥāṣil mī shawand ?	Pa de mulk ke kūm kūm (*rasad*) *tsizūna* milyā kegī.
50 There is *wheat*, Indian corn, barley and fruit.	*Gehūn*, jawār, jau aur mewajāt haiṅ.	*Gandum*, jawār, jau wa aṣmār hastand.	Ghanam, juwār, orbushe au mewe dī.
51 There is *dāl*, rice and *lucerne*.	*Mūng*, chāṅwal aur *shaftal* haiṅ.	*Māsh* birinj wa *shaftal* hast.	*Dāl*, shole au *shantala* dah.
52 They *have sown* the wheat, but it has not *sprouted* yet.	Gehūṅ *boe haiṅ* magar abhī *uge* nahīṅ.	Gandum *kāshta and* magar hinoz na *barāmada* ast.	Ghanam ye karelī dī wale tar osa zarghona shawī na dī.

English.	Urdū.	Persian.	Pashtū.
53 The barley is green, but the rice is nearly ripe.	Jau sabz hai lekin dhān ḳarīb pakne kā hai.	Jau sabz ast lekin shālī nazdīk ba pukhtan ast.	Orbushe shne dī wale shole lau ta nizhde dē.
54 All the men *are ploughing.*	Sab admī *hal jotte* haiṅ.	Hama mardumān *ḳulba mī rānand.*	Tol saṛī *yawī kawī.*
55 Can you *collect* corn for one thousand horses, and flour for three thousand soldiers?	Tum yahāṅ dāna hazār ghoṛoṅ ke waste *jama' kar* sakte ho aur ātā tīn hazār sipāhiyoṅ ke wāste?	Shumā mī tawāned ki barāe yak hazār aspān dāna *jama'* kuned wa barāe si hazār sipāhī ārd?	Tuh da zar āsūno da pāra dāna au da dre zaro spayāno da pāra oṛuh tola wulai she.
56 Is there a well in the village? has it steining (brick lining) or not?	Gāṅw men koi kūā hai? pakkā hai yā kachchā.	Ba dih chāh ast? pukhta ast yā khām?	Pa kalī ke kūm yo koyai shto? pokh dai ka kacha?
57 How *deep* is the water?	Pānī kitnā *gahrā hai?*	Åb chi kadar *'amīḳ* ast?	Obuh tsomra *zhaware* dī?
58 If many men draw from it, does it lower the water much?	Agar bahutse ādmī us se pānī leṅ to bahut kam na hogā?	Agar bisyār kasān az ān āb bigīrand bisyār kam na khwāhad shud?	Ka der saṛī tre obuh wākhlī der kūzegī?
59 Is the water clean and cool? is it good to drink?	Pānī ṭhandā aur ṣāf hai? pīne ke wāsṭe achchhā hai?	Ab khunak o ṣāf ast? barāe khụrdan khūb ast?	Obuh saṛe au pāke dī? tsakalo la khe dī?
60 The water is not fit for cooking with or for drinking.	Yih pānī khāne pakāne aur pīne ke wāste achchhā na hīn.	Īn āb barāe pukhtan i tu 'ām o noshīdan khūb nest.	Da obuh da pakhlī au da tskalo da pāra khe na dī.
61 Where is the spring?	Chashma kahāṅ hai?	Chashma kujā ast?	Chīna cherta dah?
62 Is there water all the year round? *does* it *flow* all the hot weather?	Yahāṅ pānī hamesha rahtā hai? tamām garmī meṅ *bahtā hai?*	Īnjā āb mudām mī manad? bagarmī *mī ravad?*	Tamām kāl dalta mudām obuh wī? pa tol oṛī ke *bahegī.*

English.	*Urdū.*	*Persian.*	*Pashtū.*
63 How far is it to the next place where there is water ?	Yahāṅ se kitnī dūr aur pānī milegā ?	Az īnjā chand dūr jāe dīgar āb yāfta khwāhad shud ?	La de zai na bul zai chi obuh mūnde shī tsomra lare dai ?
64 The water in this well is *better* than the water in that spring.	Is kueṅ kā pānī us chashme ke pānī se *bihtar* hai.	Āb i īn chāh az āb i ān chashma *bihtar* ast.	Da dagh koī obuh de haghe chīne la obo na *khe* dī.
65 What kinds of trees are there in the forest ?	Is jangal meṅ kis ḳism ke darakht haiṅ?	Ba īn ṣaḥrā kudām kudām darakhthā hastand ?	Pa zangal ke tsa rang wune dī ?
66 There are *wild olive*, sāl, sheeshum and *mulberry;* by the river there are *willows*.	Yahān *zaitūn*, sāl, shīsham aur *shāhtūt* haiṅ ; naddī ke pās *bed majnū* haiṅ.	Īnjā *zaitūn*, sāl, shīsham wa *tūt* hastand ; nizd i rūd *bed* ast.	Dale *khauwa*, sāl, shawa an *tūtān* dī da sīnd pa ghāṛa walle dī.
67 Cut me a thick stick and a small *switch*.	Hamāre wasṭe ek moṭī lāthī aur ek chhotī *ḳamchī* kāṭo.	Barāe mā yak chob i luk wa yak *ḳamchīni* bārīk bubur.	Mā la yo lowaṛ au ywah lakhta pre ka.
68 Are there thorns on those *bushes ?*	Un *jhāṛiyoṅ* meṅ kānṭe hain ?	Ba ān *būtahā* khār hastand?	Pa hagho *būtyo* ke aghzī dī ?
69 Go on the grass and not on the road.	Ghās par chalo, saṛak par na chalo.	Bālāe kāh burau ba shāh rāh ma rau.	Pa wākho za, na pa lār.
70 Go along the foot path.	Pakdandī par jāo.	Ba rāh burau.	Pa waṛa lār za.
71 There are *snakes* in the grass and *scorpions* under the stones.	Is ghās meṅ *sāmp* haiṅ aur us patthar ke nīche *bichchhū*.	Ba īn kāh *mārān* hastand wa zer i ān sang *gazhdum*.	Pa wakho ke *mārān* au da kāṅṛo lānde laṛamān dī.
72 Is there any *danger* on this road at night ?	Rāt ko is raste meṅ *dahshat* hai ?	Ba īn rāh ba shab *khauf* ast ?	Pa shpa ke pa de lār tlal *wyara* larī ?

English.	*Urdū.*	*Persian.*	*Pashtū.*
73 If a man is armed there is no *fear*, one man should not go alone.	Agar ādmī hathyār band ho to kuchh *dahshat* nahīn, magar akelā nahīṅ jāne chāhiye.	Agar ādam aṣlaḥ dār bāshad hech *khaṭra* nest, magar tanhā raftan na bāyad.	Ka saṛai wasla larī wyara nashta wale tanhā tlal na boya.
74 When I arrive at the place where the road divides into two, which am I to take?	Jab maiṅ wāhāṅ pahunchuṅ ki jahāṅ rasta do ṭaraf ko jātā hai to maiṅ kis ṭaraf jāūn?	Waḳte ki man ba do rāhā bi rasam kudām sū birawam?	Kūm wakht chi zuh hase zai ta warsham chi lār dwa zai kegi pa kūma ba zam?
75 Shall I go to the right or to the left?	Ham dāhine ṭaraf jāeṅ yā bāeṅ?	Dast i rāst birawam yā chap?	Khī lās ta zam ka gats ta?
76 Where does the *northern* road lead to, and where the *southern?*	*Utar wālā* rastā kidhar jātā hai aur *dakkhan wālā* kidhar?	Rāh i *shimālī* ba kudām jā mī rawad wa *janūbī* kujā?	*Da bara* lār charta zī au *lara* charta?
77 Am I to turn to the *east* when I get to the top of that rising ground?	Jab maiṅ us ṭile par pahunchūṅ to *pūrab* ko phir jāūṅ?	Waḳte ki man bālāe toda bi rasam sū e *sharaḳ* bi gardam?	Kūm wakht chi zuh da ghundai sar ta wukhegam numar khāta la ba garzam?
78 After you have gone through the rice-field, turn to the east and go straight forward for two miles.	Us dhān kī khet meṅ se nikalkar pūrab kē ṭaraf phiro aur do mail tak sīdhe chale jāo.	Az ān kisht i shālī rafta simt i sharaḳ gardīda do mail rāst birawed.	Chi la sholgar na ter she numar khāta ta wugarza au barābar yo kroe wṛānde zuh.
79 When you get to the river, *swim* across the first *channel* and get on to the *island.*	Jab tum naddī par pahuncho pahle *nāle* se *pair* kar pār ho aur *tāpū* par jāo.	Waḳte ki shumā ba daryā bi rased az *shākh* i awwal *shināwarī karda* ba *jazīra* bi rased.	Chi sīnd ta wurase pa wṛambaī nāla pa lāmbo pore uza au *bele* ta warsha.
80 Will a horse sink in the *mud* here?	Is kīchaṛ meṅ ghoṛā phas jāegā?	Ba īn *khilāb* asp gharaḳ mī shawad?	Pa de khato ke ba ās khakh shī?

English.	Urdū.	Persian.	Pashtū.
81 *Will* a man *sink* in over his knees?	Ādmī ghuṭhnī tak *dhas jāegā?*	Ādam tā ba zānū *faro mī rawad?*	Saṛai ba tar zāngana pore *khakh shī?*
82 The water is up to the horse's *belly.*	Pānī ghoṛe ke *pet* tak hai.	Āb tā *shikam* i asp ast.	Obuh da ās tar kheṭe pore dī.
83 Call another man.	Dūsrā ādmī bulāo.	Shakhs i dīgar biṭalab.	Bul saṛai rāwubola.
84 Ask it from him.	Us se pūchho.	Az o bupurs.	La hagha na pokhtana wuka.
85 Where is he going to show it to him?	Wuh kidhar jātā hai ki usko dikhlāwe?	O kujā mī rawad ki ba o bi numāyad?	Hagha cherta zī chi hagha ta wur wukhayī?
86 There has been a great deal of rain in the hills.	Pahāṛoṅ par bahut sa meṅh paṛā hai.	Ba kohistān bisyār bārān shuda ast.	Pa ghrūno der bārān wareda-lai dai.
87 The river is dry in the hot season.	Yih naddī garmī meṅ khushk rahtī hai.	Īn jū ba garma khushk mī shawad.	Pa oṛī ke dā wela wuchawī.
88 Does this river *fall into* the Indus?	Yih naddī daryā e atak meṅ *miltī hai?*	Īn rūd dar abbāsīn mī rawad?	Dā sīnd pa abasīn ke *gaḍegī?*
89 It falls into the Kābul *above* Nowshera.	Naushahra ke *ūpar* daryā e Kābul men miltī hai.	*Bālā* e Naushahra dar daryā e Kābul mī uftad.	La Naukhahr na *pās* da Kābul pa sīnd ke gaḍegī.
90 It rains here in the cold weather; the river has risen.	Jāṛe ke mausim meṅ yahāṅ meṅh barastā hai; naddī chaṛh gaī hai.	Ba mausim i sarma īnjā bārish mī shawad; ba daryā sailāb ast.	Pa zhamī ke dalta bārān waregī daryāb khatalai dai.

SECTION X.—SURVEYING.

English.	Urdū.	Persian.	Pashtū.
1 Collect your party together.	Apnā madad jama' karo.	Mardumān i khudrā jama' kun.	Khpal saṛī ṭol ka.
2 Leave this *bamboo* and that stick standing.	Yih *bāṅs* aur wuh lakṛī khaṛī rahne do.	Īn *bāṅs* (*nai*) wa ān chob istāda bimāned.	Dā *darwai* au hagha largai wilār pregda.
3 They are required as *marks*.	We *nishān* ke wāsṭe chāhiye.	Anhā barāe *nishān* ba kār and.	*Nakhe da* pāra pakār dī.
4 Set up *flags* on the two *extreme* marks.	Donoṅ *sirre' ke* nishānoṅ par *jhandī* lagāo.	Ba har do nishān i *sar bairaḳ* istāda kun.	Da dwaṛo saro pa nakha *janḍa* wuderawa.
5 First cut a *line* on the ground *between* these two marks.	Pahle in donoṅ nishānoṅ ke *bīch dāgh bel* karo.	Awwal *miyān* i har do nishān *dāgh i bel* bukun.	Wṛumbai da dwāṛo nakho pa myanz ke *dāgh* wulagawa.
6 *Attach* a *cord* to that peg; now draw it tight.	Us khūntī men *ḍorī bāndho*, ab zor se khīncho.	Ba ān mekh *respān basta kun*, aknūn ba zor bikash.	Pa hagh mugi paṛai *wutaṛa* os ye ma maẓbūṭ rākāga.
7 Draw out the *tape*.	*Fītā* khīnch lo.	*Fītā* rā bikash.	*Mazai* rākāga.
8 Set up the *compass* over the heap of stones.	*Kampās* patthar ke dherī ke ūpar khaṛā karo.	*Kampās* rā ba bālā e ambār i sang istāda kun.	Da hagho kaṅro pa derī *kampās* wudarāwa.
9 Go about ten *paces beyond* the last peg, and look there if they are all in line.	Das *ḳadam* ākhir khūntī ke *pīchhe* jākar dekho ki sab khūntiān ek lakir par sīdhī haiṅ.	Dah *ḳadam pas* i mekh i i ākhir rafta bibīned ki hama mekhhā ba yak khaṭṭ hastand.	La wruste mogī na las *ḳadama wṛānde* ter sha au wugora hi ṭol sam dī ka na.
10 Place the flag exactly over the mark which I made yesterday.	Jo nishān ki maiṅ ne kal ḳiyā thīk us par jhandī lagāo.	Neza rā ba ān nishān istāda kun ki man dīroz karda būdam.	Kūma nakha chi mā parūn kaṛīda janḍa jukht pa hagha wudarawa.
11 Hold the *staff* upright.	*Gaz* ko sidhā khaṛa karo.	*Neza* rā ba'amūd barābar bigīr.	*Janḍa* sama negha wunīsa.
12 Stretch another cord in the same *manner* on this side.	Usī *ṭaraḥ* ek aur ḍorī is ṭaraf lagāo.	Hamīn *ṭaur* yak respān i dīgar ba īn sū basta kun.	Pa dā shān yo bul puṛai pa de khwā wutaṛa.

English.	Urdū.	Persian.	Pashtū.
13 Now see that the *distance* between the two cords is the same at both ends.	Ab dekhne chāhiye ki *fāṣila* doriyoṅ ke donoṅ sirre par eksān hai.	Aknūn bibīned ki *fāṣila* miyān i respānhā ba har do sar barābar ast.	Os wugora chi da dwāṛo paṛyo pa manz ke wut barābar dai.
14 Place the *rod* here. See if it touches the cord.	*Gaz* yahāṅ lagāo. Dekho ki dorī meṅ lagtā hai.	*Gaz* īnjā binih. Bibīn ki ba respān juft ast.	*Hamsa* dale kegda. Wugora chi pa paṛī lagī ka na.
15 Move it a little to the right.	Usko thoṛā dāhine ṭaraf sarkāo.	Ān rā ẕarra sū e rāst bujumban.	Hagha lag khī lās ta wugarzawa.
16 Move the other a little to the left.	Dūsre ko thoṛā baeṅ ṭaraf karo.	Dīgar rā ẕurra ba sūe chap bigardān.	Bula lag gats lās ta wugarzawa.
17 Now do the same at the other end of the cord.	Ab dorī ke us sirre par bhī aisā hī karo.	Aknūn ba dīgar sar i respān hamīṅ ṭaur kun.	Os da puṛī bul sar ham dāse ka.
18 Hold the rod at *right angles* to the line.	Gaz dorī ke *guniyā meṅ* karo.	Gaz rā *'amūd* i īn respān bukun.	Da līke pa khī guṭ hamsa wunīsa.
19 Go to the top of that hill, and place yourself so that you can see me and the two men who went in that direction, and also that tree in the *valley*.	Us pahāṛ ke ūpar jākar aise jage khaṛe ho ki jahāṅ se hamko aur un do ādmiyoṅ ko jo us ṭaraf gaye haiṅ dekho aur wuh darakht bhī jo *maidān* meṅ hai dikhaī de.	Bālāe ān koh rafta ba chunīn jāe istāda shawed ki mārā wa har do ādam rā ki ān sū raftand bibīned, wa nīz ān darakht ki ba *maidān* ast.	Da hagha ghrah tsuke ta wukhega au pa dase zai wudarega chi mā au hagha dwa saṛī chi hagha khwa lāṛal wīne au ham hagha wuna chi pa *maidān* ke dah katae she.
20 Can you see the man who went forward with a flag?	Tum ko wuh admī jo jhandī leke āge gayā dikhāī deta hai?	Ān shakhṣ rā mī bīned ki neza pesh burda ast?	Hagha saṛai chi jandaye pa makh a makh yawṛa tuh wīne?
21 Hold the staff *perfectly* upright; do not let it shake.	Gaz ko *ṭhīk* sīdhā khaṛā rakho aur mat hilne do.	Gaz rā *durust* istāda kun wa zinhār ki na jumbad.	Largai sam wunīsa khwazawa ye ma.

English.	Urdū.	Persian.	Pashtū.
22 When you are measuring you must hold the chain exactly in the place where the end of the *chain* came last time.	Jab tum paimāish karo to chāhiye ki pichhlā sirra *jarīb* kā ṭhīk agle ke jage par āwe.	Waḳte ki paimāish bukuned khiyāl dāred ki sar i pas i *jarīb* ba 'ainihi hamān jā biyāyad ki peshīna būd.	Kūm wakht chi kach kawe boya chi da kach *zanzīr* wrastanai sar pa hagha zāi kegde kūm zāi chi ye wṛumbanai sar wuh.
23 *Shake* the chain.	Jarīb ko *jhāro*.	Jarīb rā *biyafshān*.	Zanzīr *wu tsandawa*.
24 *Carry* the chain; do not *drag* it on the ground.	Jarīb ko *uṭhāke lejāo* zamīn par mat *khīncho*.	Jarīb rā bardāshta *dar dast bibar*, ba zamīn ma kashash.	Zanzīr pa lās ke wākhla pa zmoka ye ma rākāga.
25 See that there are no *kinks* in it.	Dekho ki usmeṅ koī *girih* na ho.	Bibīn ki darān *girih* na bāshad.	Wugora chi pa ke hets *ganḍe* na wī.

SECTION XI.—ARTIFICERS' WORK.

1 I am going to the works now; I will pay you when I come back.	Ham abhī kām par jāte haiṅ tumko laut kar rūpae denge.	Man aknūn ba kār mīrawam wāpas āmada rūpiya khwāham dād.	Zuh os kār ta zam chi rāwugarzam rupiye ba darkam.
2 Have you received payment *in full?*	Tum ne *kull* pā liyā?	*Shumā* be bāḳ shuda ed?	*Tole* darta milya shwe?
3 I told you *plainly* you should only get full pay on *condition* that you work hard all day.	Ham ne tum ko *ṣāf* batāyā ki tumko purī ṭalab milegī ba *sharṭe* ki tum din bhar achchhī ṭarah kām karo.	Man shumā rā *khūb* fahmānīdam ki shumā ṭalab barābar khwāhed yaft ba *sharṭe* ki tamām roz ba khūbī kārkuned.	Mā darta tsargand weyalī wū chi pūrā ṭalab ba darta hala milya kegī chi tola wraz kār kawe.

English.	*Urdū.*	*Persian.*	*Pashtū.*
4 I shall not pay you unless you finish this work before night.	Agar tum rāt se peshtar is kām ko tamām na karoge to kuchh nahīṅ milegā.	Agar shumā pesh az shām īn kār rā tamām na kuned hech na khwāhed yāft.	Ka la mākhām na wṛānde dā kār tamām na ke hets ba na mūme.
5 The *foundations* will be built with bricks in lime and the superstructure with stones in mud.	*Bunyād* īnt aur *chūne* se banegī aur ūpar kī 'imārat patthar aur gāre se.	*Bunyād* ba khisht wa *āhak* taiyār khwāhad shud wa kār i bālā ba sang o gil.	*Wekh* ba pa khikhto au *chūne* sara joṛegī au da pās kār ba pa kāṅṛo au khato sara kegī.
6 Tell the men not to throw down the bricks in that way.	Un ādmiyoṅ se kaho ki īnteṅ is ṭarah se na phenkēṅ.	Ba ān ashkhāṣ bugo ki khishthā rā īn ṭaur niyandāzand.	Saṛo ta wuwāya chi khikhte de dase na ghurzawī.
7 They must put each brick down carefully on the *stack*.	Harek īnt khabardārī se *chatte* men lagāne chāhiye.	Har yak khisht ba hoshyārī ba toda binihand.	Pa hokhyāraī sara ywah ywah khakhta pa *ḍerī* kegdī.
8 This *mortar* is too thick; it wants *more* water.	Yih *chūnā* bahut sakht hai; aur pānī chāhiye.	Īn *khamīr* i āhak bisyār sakht ast āb i ziyāda bāyad.	Dā *chūna* waghaira ḍera sakhta dah nure obuh pakār dī.
9 Mix some *hemp* with the lime for the plaster.	Plāstar ke wāsṭe chune meṅ thoṛa *san* milāo.	Barāe astarkārī ba khamir i āhak *san* biyāmez.	Da lew da pāra pa chūna ke nor *saṅṛ* gaḍ ka.
10 Spread the mortar with the *trowel* and then lay the brick.	Chūnā *karnī* se bichhā kar īnt lagāo.	Maṣālaḥ peshtar ba gilmāla hamwār karda bālāyash khisht bichaspān.	Chūna pa *karandai* sara wughoṛawa au pre pāsa khakhte wulagawa.
11 Apply the *plumb line* and square to that *corner*, and see if it is *correct*.	*Sāhul* aur gūnyā us *kone* par lagā kar dekho ki ṭhik hai.	*Sahāwal* wa ḳāima nihāda bibīned ki ān *gosha* i dīwāl *durust* ast.	*Sahūl* au ḳāima pa hagha *kunj* wulagawa au gora chi sam dai ka na.
12 Place a *ladder* at the end of the *building* that I may get on the roof.	*Makān* ke sirre par ek *siṛhī* lagāo ki ham chhat par jā sakeṅ.	Ba gosha i *makān* yak *zīna* i chobī binih ki man ba saḳf bālā shudan bitawānam.	Da *makān* pa ywuh guṭ *andarpāya* wulagawa chi zah pa kotah wukhegam.

English.	Urdū.	Persian.	Pashtū.
13 Take care that the bricks in the *arch* radiate properly.	Khabardār ki *ḍāt* kī īnteṅ chalākī meṅ lageṅ.	Hosh kun ki khishthā ē *miḥrāb* māil ba markaz bāshand.	Da *mihrāb* tole khikhte pa hokhyārai sara lagawul boya.
14 Tie a string on the *centre* and see if it is right.	Ek sūt *markaz* meṅ bāndh kar dekho ki ṭhik hai.	Yak respān ba *markaz* basta bibīn ki ṣaḥiḥ ast.	Yo mezai pa manz ke wuteṛaṅ au gora chi sam dai ka na.
15 The *wall* does not look level here.	Is jage meṅ *dīwāl pansāl* meṅ nahīṅ ma'lūm hotī.	Ba īnjā *dīwár hamwār* ma'lūm na mi shawad.	Pa de zai *dīwāl hamwār* au sam na khkarā kegi.
16 Mind you fill the *joints* well with mortar; let *none* of them be the least empty.	Khabardār ki har ek *joṛ* maṣāle se bhrā jāwe *koī* zarra khālī *na* rahe.	Khabardār ki har yak *darz* ba maṣālaḥ pur shawad wa'hech jā khālī *na* mānad.	Khabardār osa chi tol *darzūna* pa maṣālaḥ sara khah dakegī au yo ham khālī pāte na shī.
17 See if that *truss* is upright.	Dekho ki wuh *ḳainchī* sīdhī khaṛī hai.	Bibīned ki ān *ḳainchī* ba ḥālat 'amūdī bāshad.	Wugoṛa chi ḳainchī barābara wilāra wī.
18 Did you cut the wood with an *axe* or a saw?	Tum ne lakṛī *kulhāṛī* yā āre se kātī?	Shumā chob rā ba *tabar* yā arra tarāshīded?	Ta largai pa *tabar* yā pa ara sara prekaṛ?
19 You must first dress it with an *adze*, and then plane it.	Pahle *basūle* se chhīlne chāhiye aur pīchhe rande se ṣāf karnā.	Awwal ba *tesha* tarashīdan bāyad wa ba'd ba randa ṣāf kardan.	Awwal ye pa tarkhaza sara wutega byā ye randa ka.
20 *Bore a hole* with an *auger* and put a *bolt* in.	*Barme* se *chhed karkar* ek *kābila* lagāo.	Ba *barma sūrākh karda* yak *kābila* bi chaspān.	Pa *barma* sara *sūṛai wuka* au aṛamai wulagawa.
21 That wood is green; it will twist.	Wuh lakṛī gīlī hai teṛhi hojāegī.	Īn chob tar ast pechīda khwahad shud.	Ā largai lūnd dai kog ba shī.
22 Use good malleable *iron*, and file the edges.	Achchhī suchchī pattī kā *lohā* kām meṅ lāo aur kināroṅ ko retī se ṣāf karo.	*Āhan* i kuft pazīr ba kār biyār wa har baghal ash ba sohān ṣāf kun.	Khah khwaga *ospana* wulagawa au tsanḍe ye sohān ka.
23 The thread of that *screw* is not cut deep enough.	Us *pech* kī chūṛī khūb gahrī nahīṅ.	Shigāf i pech i ān mekh khūb 'amīk nest.	Da hagh *pech* manz khuh zhawar na dai.

English.	*Urdū.*	*Persian.*	*Pashtū.*
24 Don't dig there.	Wahāṅ mat khodo.	Ānjā ma kan.	Halta ma kana.
25 How many men are digging?	Kitne ādmī khodte haiṅ ?	Chand nafar mī kanand ?	Tso saṛī kanī.
26 *Dig* a little deeper.	Zarra aur gahrā *khodo.*	Zarra 'amīktar *bikan.*	Lag ziyāt zhawar *wukana.*
27 How deep is the digging ?	Khodāī kitnī gahrī hai ?	Khandaḳ chand 'amīḳ ast ?	Khandaḳ tsomra zhawar dai ?
28 Lay down the *spade* on the ground.	*Belcha* zamīn par rakh do.	*Belcha* ba zamīn bi nih.	Yūm pa zmaka kegda.
29 Is there no *handle* to this spade ?	Is belcha meṅ *dasta* nahīṅ ?	Īn bel *dasta* na dārad.	Da dagh yama *lāstai* nashta ?
30 This handle is loose; put it right.	Yih dasta ḍhīlā hai; usko durust karo.	Īn dasta narm ast ān rā durust kun.	Dā lāstai khwazegī maẓbūṭ ye ṭak waha.
31 Put in a small *pin* of wood at this end.	Ek chhotī lakṛī kī *mekh* is sirre men lagāo.	Yak chobīn *mekh i* khurd ba īn sar bichaspān.	Da largī yo narai totanai pa de sar ṭak waha.
32 Are the rest of the men all at work ?	Aur sab ādmī kām par haiṅ ?	Dīgar hama mardumān ba kār ḥāẓir and ?	Nor ṭol saṛī kār kawī ?
33 How many men went to the first work ?	Pahle kām par kitne ādmī gae ?	Ba kār i awwal chand nafar raftand ?	Pa wṛumbī kār tso saṛī laṛal ?
34 They are too *close*, there is not room for both.	We bahut *nazdīk* haiṅ donoṅ ke wasṭe jagah nahīṅ.	Eshān bisyār *mutaṣṣil* and barāe har do jāe nest.	Daī ḍer *nizhde* dī da 'dwāṛo zāī nashta.
35 Begin from this mark.	Is nishān se shurū' karo.	Az īn nishān shurū' kun.	La de nakhe kār shurū' ka.
36 Take off this *branch*, this which *droops* over head.	Is *tahnī* ko kāṭo yih jo sir ke ūpar *latkī hai.*	In *shākh* rā ki bālāe sar *āwezān ast* bu bur.	Dā tsānga preka, dā chi pa sar de zwaṛanda dah.
37 What kind of *soil* is there at that place ?	Us jage kis ḳism kī *miṭṭī* hai ?	Ānjā kudām ḳism i *gil* ast ?	Da hagh zāī tsa rang *khāwra* dah.
38 Where was this *stiff clay* got from ?	Yih *chiknī miṭṭī* kahān se milī ?	Īn *gil i charb* kujā yāfta ṣhud ?	Dā *zīga khāwra* da cherta munda ?

English.	Urdū.	Persian.	Pashtū.
39 This is only *sand.*	Yih ṣirf *ret* hai.	Īn ṣirf *reg* ast.	Dā sirp *shoge* dī.
40 Here a *pickaxe* is necessary.	Yahāṅ *gaintī* chāhiye.	Īnjā *kulang* mī bāyad.	Dalta *genṭaī* pa kār dah.
41 The *wheel* of this barrow is loose.	Is hāth gāṛhī kā *paihyā* ḍhīlā hai.	*Charkh* i īn gardūn narm ast.	Da de lās gāḍī *pāya* narma dah.
42 This *rammer* is very light; a heavier one will be necessary.	Yih *dūrmaṭ* bahut halkā hai; is se bhārī chāhiye.	Īn gilkob bisyār subuk ast azīn sangīntar bāyad.	Dā *durmaṭ* ḍer spak dai la de na bul drūnd pakār dai.
43 Bring a *basket*, a square and a tape.	*Ṭokrī*, gunyā aur fītā lāo.	*Sabd*, ḳāima wa fītā biyār.	*Ṭokrai*. chār kunjai au mazai rāwṛa.
44 Throw the *earth* into this ravine.	*Miṭṭī* is nāle men ḍālo.	*Gil* ba in jū biyandāz.	*Khāwra* pa de lakhtī ke wugharzawa.
45 What sort of soil did you find in digging that hole?	Us gaṛhe ke khodne meṅ kaisī miṭṭī milī?	Az kandīdan i ān ghār chi ṭaure gil bar āmad?	Chi ā sūraī de kanda tsa rang khāwra de mūnda?
46 Can you show me the place?	Tum hamko jagah dikhā sakte ho?	Mārā jā nīshān dādan mī tawāned?	Māla ā zāi khayalai she?
47 Not just now; there is too much water there.	Abhī nahīṅ wahāṅ pānī bahut hai.	Hanoz na chirā ki ānjā āb bisyār ast.	Os na zaka chi halta ḍere obuh dī.
48 Collect all the tools.	Sab hathyār jama' karo.	Hama asbāb jāma' kun.	Ṭol kālī ṭol ka.
49 Did the chaprassi shew you my marks?	Chaprāsī ne hamare nishān tumko dikhāe?	Chaprāsī nishān i mārā ba shumā namūd?	Chaprāsī dzmā nakhe dar ta wu khayale?
50 Do not cut *perpendicular; conform* to the slope of the wall.	*Sīdhā* mat kāto; dīwāl kī salāmē ke *muwāfiḳ karo.*	'*Amūdan* ma tarāsh *muwāfiḳ* i salāmī i dīwār *kun.*	*Negh* ma kana, da dīwāla pa shān ye salāmī ka.
51 Measure a foot and a half.	(Hāthbhar) deṛh fut nāpo.	Yak o nīm fūt (yak dast) paimā ish kun.	Yo nīm fūt (yo lās) kach ka.

English.	Urdū.	Persian.	Pashtū.
52 The *excavation* will be two and a half feet deep at that end and three and a quarter at this end.	*Khodāī* kī gahrāī us sirre par aṛhāī fut aur is sirre par sawā tīn fut hogī.	'Amaḳ i *khandaḳ* ba ān sar do wa nīm fūt wa ba īn sar si fut wa yak chahārum i fut mī bāyad.	Da hagh tsang zhawartya ba dwa nīm au da dagh tsang pāo bānde dre fūta wī.
53 When you have finished the bank, *plant* grass all over it.	Jab tum pushta taiyār kar chuko tab us par ghās *jamāo.*	Waḳte ki pushta rā taiyār kuned bālāyash kāh *bikāred.*	Chi la ghāṛe joṛawalo na wuzgār shè wākha pre wukaṛa.
54 How many days do the bricks take to dry?	Kitne dinoṅ meṅ īnt sūkhegī?	Ba chand roz khishthā khūshk mīshawand?	Khakhte pa tso wrazo ko wuchegī?
55 If there be many clouds they dry slowly.	Agar bādal bahut ho to deri se sūkhegī.	Agar abr bisyār bāshad ba der khushk khwāhand shud.	Ka ḍere wryaze wī no pa dero wrazo ke wuchegī.
56 In how many days will the bricks be ready for the *kiln?*	Kitne dinoṅ meṅ īnteṅ *bhaṭṭī* ke wāsṭe taiyār hongīṅ?	Ba chand roz khishthā barāe *pazāwa* taiyār khwāhand shud?	Khakhte ba pa tso wrazo ke *pajāwe* la taiyāre shī?
57 They shrink much in burning.	Pakne meṅ ghaṭ jātī haiṅ.	Az pukhtan dar pazāwa khurd mī shawand.	Ā pa swo ke kamegī.
58 Where does the wood for the kilns come from?	Lakṛī bhaṭṭī ke wāste kahān se ātī hai?	Hezm barāe pazāwa az kujā mī āyad?	Pajāwo la largī la kūm zāi na rāzī?
59 How much wood is required for one thousand bricks?	Hazār īnt ke wāsṭe kitnī lakṛī chāhiye?	Barāe yak hazār khisht chi ḳadar hezm bāyad?	Yo zar khakhto da pāra tsomra largī pa kār dī?
60 *Arrange* the bricks carefully in the kiln.	Bhaṭṭī meṅ īnt *khabardārī se bharo.*	Khisht dar pazāwa *ba hoshyārī bīnih.*	*Pa hokhyārī* au tartib sara khakhte pa pazāwa ke *kegda.*

English.	Urdū.	Persian.	Pashtū.
61 Place the bricks in the lower *layers* on edge at small intervals.	Nīche ke *raddoṅ* meṅ īṅteṅ nazdīk nazdik kharī karo.	Ba *tah* i zerīn khishthā rā nazdīk nazdīk istāda kun.	Pa kūz tah ke khakhte nizhde nizhde wudarawa.
62 In the upper layers place them *flat* and close together.	Ūpar ke raddoṅ meṅ unko *paṛī* aur milākaṛ rakho.	Ba tah i bālā ānhā rā *uftāda* wa āmekhta binih.	Pa pās rado ke ye paṛmakh zwaṛende kegda.
63 These bricks are underburnt; they are quite *yellow*.	Ye īnteṅ kam pakkī haiṅ; bilkull *pīlī* haiṅ.	Īn khishthā khūb pukhta nestand bi-ul-kull *zard* and.	Dā khakhte khe pakhe na dī, bekhī zyaṛe dī.
64 These are hard and ring well.	Ye sakht haiṅ aur achchhī āwāz detī haiṅ.	Īnhā sakht and wa āwāz i khūb mī dihand.	Dā sakhte dī au khah tanṛahār ye khegī.
65 They are quite red throughout.	Ye andar bāhar se khūb surkh haiṅ.	Īn derūn o berūn khūb surkh and.	Dā bekhī sre dī.
66 Burn the other bricks with *manure and litter*.	Aur īnteṅ *khāt aur kūṛe* se pakāo.	Dīgar khishthā ba *khas o khāshāk* pukhta kun.	Nore khakhte pa *ghushayo au khazalo* pakhe ka.
67 This soorkhee is not fine enough.	Yih surkhī khūb mahīn nahīṅ.	In sūrkhī khūb bārīk nest.	Dā surkhaī khah maida na dah.
68 Have you a *screen* for sifting the soorkhee.	Tumhāre pās *chhānnā* surkhī chhānne ke wāsṭe hai?	Pesh i shumā *ghirbāl* barāe bekhtan i surkhī ast?	Da surkhaī chaṅṛawulo parwezai lare?
69 The ground is very sandy at that place. We must first lay down a layer of broken bricks.	Us jage zamīn bahut retlī hai: pahle ek raddā khoā dālne chāhiye.	Ān zamīn regdār ast: awwal yak tah i khishtreza andākhtān mī bayad.	Ā zmaka ā zai dera shaglana dah, awwal ywa tah da khakhto da toṭo gdal boya.
70 Have you got all the *tools* you require?	Tumhāre pās *hathyār* jitne chāhiye haiṅ?	Pesh i shumā *asbāb* i ẓarūrī maujūd ast?	Tsomra *kālī* chi pakār dī, tol darzakha shta?

English.	*Urdū.*	*Persian.*	*Pashtū.*
71 Take four or five men from the work, and go and fetch the spades.	Chār pānch ādmī kām se lekar belche lāo.	Chahār panj kas az kār burda bel biyār.	La kāra tsalor pīnza saṛī da zān sara boza au belche rāwṛa.
72 Have you sent any one to *inquire* whether we can get the *carts?*	Tum ne koī ādmī bhej dīyā *pūchhne* ke wāste ki hamko *gāṛhī* milengī yā na ?	Shumā kase rā barāe *pursīdan* firistāded ki *'araba* khwāhem yāft yā na ?	Tā *pukhtane* lā tsok legalai dai chi mūng la ba *gaḍai* milyā shī ka na ?
73 A good deal of *damage* has been done to that bridge by the *flood.*	*Sailāb* se us pul ko bahut *nukṣān* hūā.	Az *sailāb* ba ān pul bisyār *nukṣān* rasīd.	La nīz na haghe pul ḍer *nukṣānī* shawai dai.
74 *Examine* both bridges and see if the *piers* have sunk at all.	Donoṅ pul *mulāhaza karkar* daryāft karo ki *pāe* to nahīṅ dube.	Har do pul rā *mulāhaza namūda* daryāft kun ki *pāīhā* ḳadare faro rafta and yā na.	Dwāṛa pulūna khah wugora chi da *pīlpaye* khpe kho lānde shawī na dī.
75 The *parapets* of both bridges are broken.	Donoṅ puloṅ kī *manḍerī* tūṭī haiṅ.	*Dīwārhā* e parda i har do pul shikasta and.	Da pulūno da *dīwār* tsanḍe māte shawī dī.
76 The *beams* of the wooden bridge have been washed away.	Lakṛī ke pul ke *shāhtīr* bahgae haiṅ.	*Tīrhā* e pul i chobī āb burd shuda and.	Da largo da pul *shahtīrūna* obu wuṛī dī.
77 Fasten the planks down with large nails.	Takhte baṛe mekh se lagāo.	Ba takhtahā mekh i kalān bi zan.	Pa takhto loe mekhūna ṭak waha.
78 Send for the *potter* who made tiles last year.	Jis *kumhār* ne pichhle sāl khapre banāe usko bulāo.	Ān *kulāl rā* ki sāl i guzashta sifālbā taiyār karda būd bitalbān.	Hagha *kulāl* chi paros kāl ye kapre joṛe kaṛī we rāwubola.
79 Do you want flat *tiles* or half round ?	Tumko *khapre* yā nariye chahiye ?	Shumā rā *sifāl* i hamwār yā nīm mudawwar mī bāyad ?	Tuh same *kapre* ghwāṛe ka da nīme dāire ?

English.	Urdū.	Persian.	Pashtū.
80 I want some stones for the *floor*, large, flat and *thin*.	Hamko kuchh patthar *farsh* ke wāsṭe chāhiye baṛe, chauras aur *patle*.	Mārā chand sanghā barāe *farsh* mī bāyad ki darāz hamwār o *bārīk* bāshand.	Mā la tso kāṉṟe *farsh* la pakār dī, boya chi loi, sam, au *narī* wī.
81 Make a rebate on the edge of the door with a *chisel*.	Kewāṛ ke kināre par *rukhānī* se patām banāo.	Ba kināra i darwāza ba iskana jarī bisāz.	Da darwāze pa kināra pa tswarlī sara patām wuka.
82 Do not drop the glass, or it will break.	Shīshā mat girāo ṭūṭ jāegā.	Zinhār ki shīsha niyuftad wa na shikanad.	K͟hīk͟ha ma ghurzawa māta ba shī.
83 There is a *crack* in the roof of that Police Station.	Us thānne ke chhat men *darz* hūī.	Ba saḳf i ān kotwālī *darz* shuda ast.	Da haghe tsaukai pa chat ke yo *darz* dai.
84 You must take off the mud and renew the *matting*.	Miṭṭī ko utār kar nāī *chaṭāī* lagāo.	Gil bar dāshta *boriyā* e nau biyandāz.	K͟hāwra tre lare ka nawai *pūzai* prewāchawa.
85 When you put new mud on beat it well.	Jab nāī miṭṭī dālo to k͟hūb kūṭo.	Waḳte ki gil i nau biyandāzed k͟hūb bukobed.	Chi nawai gorāgil pre wāchawe k͟hah ye wuṭakawa.
86 There is not enough chopped straw in the mud plaster.	Kachche plāstar meṅ bhūsā kam hai.	Dar gil subūs kam ast.	Pa k͟hatā ke būs kam dī.
87 Take down the *ceiling* cloths, mend and wash them.	*Chhat* gīre utārkar marammat karo aur dho.	*Saḳf* parda faro awurda wa marammat karda bushoyash.	Da *chat* kapṛa kūzā ka, wu ye ganḍa au wuyewinzā.
88 Get strong *scaffolds* and brushes ready for the whitewashing.	Mazbūṭ *ṣandalī* aur kūchī sufedī ke waṣte lāo.	*Ṣandalī* e mazbuṭ o kūchī barāe sufedi biyār.	Mazbūṭe *anderpāye* au kūchaī sufaidaī la rāwṛa.
89 Whitewash one room at a time.	Sufedī har ek kamare meṅ ba'd ek dūsre ke karo.	Awwal yak yak ḥujra ba yak bār sufedī kun.	Ywah ywah ḥujra pa wār kawai.
90 Do not splash the whitewash over the trusses or the window *frames*.	Sufedī ke dāgh ḳainchī aur khiṛkī ke *chokhat* par na lagāo.	Dāgh i sufedī bāla e chob i ḳainchī wa darīcha miyandāz.	Pa ḳainchaī au da kaṛkai pa darshal chūna ma tsatsawa.

English.	Urdū.	Persian.	Pashtū.
91 When you have finished you must clean all the wood-work perfectly.	Jab kām taiyār ho to sab lakṛiyoṅ ko achchhī ṭarah ṣāf karo.	Wakte ki kār tamām shawad bāyad ki hama chobhā rā ba khūbī sāf kuned.	Chi la sufedai na wuzgār shai, ṭole darshale waghaira khe pāke kaī.
92 Bring fresh lime from the kiln, and slake it here for three days.	Tāza chūnā bhattī se lākar is jage tīn din tak *bhigā rahne do*.	Āhak i tāza az pazāwa āwurda īnjā tā si roz *khamīr bi mānad*.	La batai na nawī chūna rāwra au tar dre wrazo pore ye dalta lamda pregda.
93 Put a layer of dry grass under the mud plaster.	Kachcha plāstar ke nīche sūkhā ghās bichhāo.	Zer i gilkārī e (plāstar i) khām kāh i khushk bugustarāned.	Da goragil lānde tsah lūkha yā wuchwākha wāchawa.
94 You must scrape all the old plaster off these Barracks, and apply *cow-dung wash*.	Sab purānā plāstar in Bārakoṅ se kurch kar *gobarī* līpo.	Hama astarkārī e kuhna azīn bārakhā khārāshida bālāyash *sirgīn* bimāled.	La bārakuno na tol zoṛ lew wutogai au *gobar ye* kṛa.
95 Fill the holes in the floor with broken bricks, and *ram* them well.	Jo farsh meṅ gaṛhe haiṅ roṛoṅ se bharkar *kūṭo*.	Ghārhā ki ba farsh hastand ba khishtreza pur karda *bukobān*.	Pa talī da kote ki chi tsomra sūṛe dī ṭol la roṛo dak ka au khah ye wuṭakawa.
96 Bring a pair of compasses and a *ruler*.	Parkār aur *misṭar* lāo.	Parkār o *misṭar* biyār.	Parkār au *misṭar* rāwṛa.
97 Cut this stick with a *penknife*.	Yih lāthī *chāḳū* se kāṭo.	Īn chob ba *chāḳū* bubur.	Dā lakhta pa *chāḳū* preka.
98 Saw this *board* in two, and *pare* the edge with a chisel.	Is *takhte* ko āre se do tukṛe karo aur kināra rukhānī se *chhīlo*.	Īn *takhta* rā ba āra do pāra karda sar ash ba iskana bitarāsh.	Da *takhta* pa āre dwa tote ka au tsanḍe ye pa tswarlī sara wutega.
99 Mend the *lid* of the box and put a new lock.	Us ṣandūḳ kā *ḍhaknā* marammut karkar nayā tālā lāgāo.	*Takhta i bālā* e ān ṣandūḳ rā marammat karda ḳufl i nau bi chaspānash.	Da hagh ṣandūḳ *pās takhta* marammat ka au nawī jandra pre wulagawa.
100 Cut down the tree with an axe.	Peṛ ko kulhāṛī se kāṭ dālo.	Darakht rā ba tabar bubur.	Wuna pa tabar sara preka.

English.	Urdū.	Persian.	Pashtū.
101 I asked for a nail, not a ***needle.***	**Ham ne ek preg māṅgā *sūi* nahīṅ.**	Man yak me<u>kh</u> <u>kh</u>wāstam na *sozan.*	**Mā yo me<u>kh</u> <u>gh</u>u<u>kh</u>t na *stan.***
102 Bring the *scissors,* some screws and an auger.	*Ḳainchī,* koī pech aur barma lāo	*Miḳrāẓ* wa chand pech wa barma biyār.	*Byātī* au tso pechūna au barma ıāwṛa.

SECTION XII—MILITARY TERMS.

English.	Urdū.	Persian.	Pashtū.
1 When was the *regiment* raised?	Yih *palṭan* kab khaṛī hūī?	Īn paltan (*dasta i sipāh*) kai muḳarrar shud?	Dā *palṭan* kala wudare da?
2 How long is it since you *enlisted?*	Tum kitnī muddat se *naukar ho?*	Shumā az chand muddat *mulāzim hasted?*	Tuh da tso mude *nokar ye.*
3 I *have served* seven years in this regiment.	Maiṅ ne sāt baras is palṭan men *naukrī kī.*	Man az haft sāl ba īn paltan *mulūzim hastam.*	Zuh la owo kālo na pa de palṭan ke *nokar yam.*
4 What is his rank in the *army?*	Uskā 'uhdā *fauj* meṅ kyā hai?	O dar *fauj* chi 'uhda dārad?	Pa faudz ke da duh tsa 'uhda dah.
5 One havildar and ten men are to be on *duty* to-night in the fort.	Ek havildār aur das sipāhī āj rāt ḳil'e kī *naukrī* par hoṅge.	Yak havildār wa dah sipāhī im shab ba *ta'aiyanātī* e ḳila' <u>kh</u>wāhand būd.	Da ywuh havildār au da las spāyāno *nokarī* ba nau shpa pa ḳil'a ke lagī.
6 There are twelve men in the *guard,* and it furnishes four sentries.	Bāra sipāhī *gārḍ* meṅ haiṅ aur chār pahra dete haiṅ.	Doāzdā sipāhī ba *ṭilāya* hastand wa chahār pāsbānī mīkunand.	Pa *gārat* dwolas spayān dī au tsalor pārà warkawī.

English.	Urdū.	Persian.	Pashtū.
7 The *hammer* of your rifle is *dirty*.	Tumhārī bandūḳ kā *ghoṛā mailā* hai.	*Farzūl* i tufang i rakhdār i shumā *chirkīn* ast.	Stā da ṭopak *kolang khīran* dai.
8 How is it that my sword is *rusty?*	Hamārī kirich kis ṭaraḥ *mailī* hūī?	Shamshīr am chi ṭaur *zangdār* shud?	Tūra me tsa rang *khīrana au zangdāra* shwa.
9 That rifle will carry 1000 paces.	Wuh bandūḳ hazār ḳadam mārtī hai.	An bandūḳ hazār ḳadam mī zanad.	Hagha ṭopak pa zar ḳadama wishtal kawī.
10 Clean the inside of the *barrel*, and see that the *nipple* is clean.	*Nāl* andar se ṣafā karo aur dekho ki *topīdān* ṣāf hai.	*Nal* i tufang rā az derūn ṣāf kun wa bibīn ki *patākhī dān* ṣāf ast.	Da ṭopak shpelaī pāka ka au wugora chi da ranjak zāiye ṣāf dai.
11 Bring the bullet-mould and *lead*, to *cast* some bullets.	Sāncha aur *sīsā* golī *banāne* ke wāsṭe lāo.	Ḳālib wa *sīsā* barāe *sākhtan* i golī biyār.	Ḳālab au *sika* golai *joṛawulu* la rāwṛa.
12 Draw your scimitar from its *scabbard*.	Apnī talwār *miyān* se nikālo.	Shamshīr i khud ra az *miyān* bikash.	Khpula tūra la toke wubāsa.
13 How many *cartridges* have you in your pouch?	Tumhāre tostdān meṅ kitne *kārtūs* haiṅ.	Ba tostdān i shumā chand *wuzun* hastand?	Pa toshdān (kīsa) ke da tso *kartūsūna* dī?
14 Give me the *waist-belt* and *cross-belt*.	Hamko *petī* aur *partalā* do.	Mārā *kamarband* o *partala* bidih.	*Petai* au *partala* rāka.
15 Fasten the flag to a *lance* and plant it on the top of the tower.	Jhandī ko ek *barche* meṅ bāndh kar us burj ke ūpar khaṛa karo.	Bairak rā ba *neza* basta bālāe ān burj istāda kun.	Janda pa *naize* porai wutaṛa au da burz pa sar ye khakha ka.
16 Bring some shot and powder for the *artillery*.	*Topkhāne* ke wāsṭe thoṛe gole aur bārūt lāo.	Barāe *topkhāna* golahā wa bārūd biyār.	*Topkhāne* da pāra golai au dārū rāwṛa.
17 The wheels of that gun-carriage are *weak* and the *axle* is cracked.	Us top kī petī ke paihiyē *kam zor* haiṅ aur *dhu* rā phatā hūā hai.	Charkhhāe (i'rābahāe) ān top *kam zor* hastand wa *mil* shikasta ast.	Da top da gāḍī pāye *kamzore* dī au *dura ye* chāwdalī dah.

English.	Urdū.	Persian.	Pashtū.
18 The regiment must march an hour before daybreak.	Ek ghanṭā peshtar fajr se palṭan kūnch karegī.	Yak sā'aṭ pesh az subḥ sipāh kūch khwāhad kard.	Da saba kido na ywah ganta wṛānde paltana ba rawāna shī.
19 When you are within two hundred paces of the *enemy*, *charge*.	Jab tum se *dushman* do sau ḳadam par rahe tab *ḍhāwā karo*.	Waḳte ki *ḥasūd* az shumā ba do sad ḳadam bi mānad *ḥamla kuned*.	Chi *dukhman* dwa sawa ḳadama lere wī pre *ḥalla kai*.
20 *Load* your pistol and shoot that *mutineer*.	Apnā pistol *bharkar* us *bāghī* ko māro.	Tufangcha i khud *pur karda* āu *bāghī* rā bukush.	Tamāncha *dakaka* au pre hagha *yāghī*wuwala.
21 He is a traitor.	Wuh namak ḥarām hai.	O namak ḥarām ast.	Hagha namak ḥarām dai.
22 The hill men *attacked* the *caravan*.	Pahārī logoṅ ne *ḳāfile* par *ḥamla kīya*.	Mardumān i kohī ba *ḳāfila ḥamla kardand*.	Da ghrah khalḳo pa *kārwān* halla wukṛa.
23 After firing two rounds they *fled*.	Ba'd do do golī mārne ke we *bhāge*.	Ba'd az sar kardan i do do golī *gurekhtand*.	Chi dwa dazūna ye wukṛa no *wutakhtedal*.
24 Two *corporals* were wounded and one soldier killed.	Do *nāik* zakhmī hūe aur ek sepāhī mārā gayā.	Do *nāik* zakhmī shudand wa yak sipāhī kushta shud.	Dwa *nāikān* ghobal au yo spāi pa ṭūro shuh.
25 One is *dangerously* and the other *slightly* wounded.	Ek *kārī* zakhmī hai aur ek *khafīf*.	Yak zakhm i *kārī* khurda ast wa dīgar *khafīf*.	Yo *ḍer sakht* zhobal dai au bul lag.
26 The enemy *was* completely *defeated*.	Dushman ko bi-l-kull *shikast* dī gaī.	Dushman bi-ul-kull *shikast khwurd*.	Dukhman pūra mātī wukhwāṛa.
27 The *victory* is ours.	*Jīt* hamārī hai.	*Fatḥ* az mā ast.	Barai dzamūng dai.
28 The musicians are beating the drums and playing the trumpets.	Bājewāle dol mārte aur ḳarnā bajāte haiṅ.	Sarod nawāzān (muṭribān) duhul mī zanand wa ḳarnā-hā mī nawāzand.	Damān dolūna wahī au karnāe ghagawī.

	English.	*Urdū.*	*Persian.*	*Pashtū.*
29	When the regiment marches, raise the parapet of the fort, and make loop-holes in it.	Jab palṭan kūnch karegī ḳil'e kā sīnapanāh aur ūnchā karo aur us meṅ rande banāo.	Wakṭe ki paltan kūch kunad sīnapanāh i kila' ziyāda buland kun wa tīrkash bisāz.	Kūm wakht chi paltan kūch shī nu sīnapanāh uchat ka au pa ke morcha joṛa ka.
30	Dig the intrenchments opposite to the enemy's battery.	Morchāl ko dushman ke morche he sāmhne khodo.	Morchāl rā rūbarūe morcha e dushman bikan.	Morchāl da dukhman de morche pa maḳhā makh wukana.

SECTION XIII.—SICKNESS AND REMEDIES.

	English	Urdū	Persian	Pashtū
1	He fell down and cut his *forehead.*	Wuh girā is sabab se *māthā* zakhmī hūā.	O uftād o *peshānī* ash zakhmī shud.	Hagha prewut au *tandai* ye zakhmī shuh.
2	He has the *liver* complaint.	Usko *jigar* kī bīmarī hai.	O āzār i *jigar* dārad.	Da hagha pa *īna* ke khalal dai.
3	The men of this village suffer from *fever* and rheumatism.	Is gāṅw meṅ bīmarī *bukhār* aur bāī kī hai.	Ba īn dih bīmarī e *tap* o rīh mī shawad.	Pa de kilī ḳe da *tabe* au da bād ranz dai.
4	What are the prevailing diseases here? What is the matter with you?	Is mulk meṅ kaunsī bīmārīyāṅ bahut hotī haiṅ? tumko kyā bīmārī hai?	Ba īn mulk kudām maraẓhā bisyār mi shawand? shumārā kudām maraẓ ast?	Pa de zāi ke kūma kūma bīmārī zyāta kegī? da tā tsa ranz dai?
5	How long have you been *ill?*	Tum kitnī muddat se *bīmār* ho.	Az chand muddat *bīmār* hasted?	Tsomra muda shawī dah chi *nājoṛ* ye?
6	How did the illness *commence?*	Bimārī kī *ibtidā* kaisī thī?	*Ibtidā* e bīmārī chi ṭaur būd?	Ranz wṛumbai tsuh rang gaḍ shuh?

English.	Urdū.	Persian.	Pashtū.
7 Have you any head*ache ?*	Kuchh sir men *dard* hai ?	Ba sar *dard* ast ?	Sar da *khogegī ?*
8 I have fever and pains in my limbs.	Mujhe bukhār aur a'ẓā shikanī hai.	Mārā bukhār o ā'ẓāe shikanī hast.	Zah tabe nīwalai yam au ṭol badan me khogegī.
9 What other symptoms have you ?	Aur kyā kyā nishānī bīmārī ke haiṅ ?	Dīgar kudām kudām 'alāmat i maraẓ ast?	Da ranz de nare kūme nakhe dī ?
10 I have *diarrhœa*, and *vomited* three times this morning.	Mujhe *dast* āte haiṅ aur subḥ se tīn daf'a *ḳai kiya.*	Mārā *shikamrau* ast wa az subḥ si bār *istifrāgh shud.*	Rā la *dastūna* rāzī au la sabāī na me dre zalla *ḳai kaṛai dai.*
11 Have you any pain in your *stomach ?*	Tumhāre *pet* meṅ kuchh dard hai ?	Ba *shikam i* shumā dard ast ?	*Geḍa* de khogegī ?
12 When I touch you here do you feel any *pain ?*	Jab ham yahāṅ hāth lagate haiṅ to tumko *dard* ma'lūm hotā hai?	Wakte ki man īnjā dast mī niham *dard* ma'lūm mī shawad ?	Chi dar bānde lās waham khogegī ?
13 That does not hurt me.	Ūs se kuchh dard nahīṅ.	Az ān hech dard nest.	Pade na khogegam.
14 That pains very much.	Us se dard bahut hotā hai.	Az īn bisyār dard mī shawad.	Dā me ḍer khogâwī.
15 Have you any pain in your liver, or any *cough ?*	Tumhāre kaleje meṅ kuchh dard hai, yā *khāṅsī* hai ?	Ba kaleja i shumā dard ast, yā *sulfa* ast ?	Pa īna ke de tsa dard dai, ka *tukhai ?*
16 I have suffered three days from constipation, and the *purgative* I took yesterday was of no use.	Mujhko tīn roz se pāekhāna nahīṅ āyā aur jo *jalāb* maiṅ ne kal pīyā us se kuchh fāida nahiṅ hūā.	Mārā az si roz ḳabẓ ast wa az ān *mushil* ki dīroz khwurdam hech fāida na shud.	Mā la dre wrazo na loe baul nadī kaṛī au hagha *jāṛ* chi mā parūn wukhwaṛal nā kāra wū.
17 That man has a cold and rheumatism.	Us admī ko zukām aur bāī hai.	Ān shakhṣ rā ẓukām o rīh ast ?	Hagha saṛai saṛa wahalai au bād nīwalai dai.
18 That sore was caused by *cautery.*	Wuh zakhm *dāgh* se hūā.	Ān zakhm az *dāgh* shuda.	Ā zakhm la *dāgh* na paida shuh.
19 Have you had any *shivering ?*	Tumko *jāṛā* āyā thā ?	Shumārā *larza* āmada būd ?	Tuh sāṛuh pa *larza* wunīwe ?

English.	Urdū.	Persian.	Pashtū.
20 I suffer from *indigestion*.	Mujhko akṣar *bad haẓmī* rahtī hai.	Mārā akṣar *bad haẓmī* mi shawad.	Dzamā akṣar *bad haẓmī* wī.
21 Let me feel your *pulse*.	*Nabẓ* dikhlao.	*Nabẓ* binumā.	N*abẓ* rāwukhāya.
22 Put out your tongue.	Jīb nikālo.	Zabān bīrūn kun.	Zhaba rā wubāsa.
23 I have sprained my ankle.	Mere *pāe* meṅ moch āyā.	*Pāyam* pech khurda ast.	Marwand me khatalai dai.
24 He has dislocated his shoulder.	Uskā *hāth* utar gayā.	*Dast* ash bar āmada ast.	Da haghuh *wulai* khatalai dai.
25 You must keep on it a *rag* wetted with cold water.	Us par ek *kapṛā* thande pānī se bhigo kar rakho.	Yak *lattā* ba āb i sard tar karda bālā yash binihed.	Ywah tsīṛra pa saṛo obo ke ḍūba ka au lamda ye wurbānde kegda.
26 Bathe it with hot water four times a day.	Garm pānī se chār daf'e ek dinmeṅ dho.	Ba āb i garm har roz chahār bār bi shoyash.	Hara wraz ye tsalor zalla pa taude oba sara wīnza.

PART III.

VOCABULARY AND INDEX.

Note.—The numbers in the second column opposite to any word indicate the Section and Phrase where it may be found in Part II., but owing to the difference of idiom it will often occur that the translation there given will not agree with that given in this Vocabulary; for instance: the Urdū for "*To have*" is given in the Vocabulary as *rakhnā*, but on referring to I. 28 it will be seen that the affix "*ke pās*," with the Verb "*To be*," is idiomatically used instead. Some English words can only be rendered by a Phrase, as the Neuter Verbs "*To hurt*" and "*To lighten*," and in these cases the reference will supply the translation. *K* stands for the Hind. *karnā*. Pers. *kardan*, Push. *kawal*, "*To do*." When a Hindī word has been used in Persian (as being current in Kābul) the letter H is affixed.

English.	*Ref.*	*Urdū.*	*Persian.*	*Pashtū.*
Able, to be	i. 69	saknā	tawānistan	shwal.
About		koī	ḳarīb	dzana, tsa.
Above	ix. 90	ūpar	bālā	pās.
Absent		g͟hair ḥāẓir	g͟hair ḥāẓir	g͟haib.
Abundant		bahut sā	ba kas̤rat	ḍer.
Accident (misfortune)		ḥādis̤a	ḥādis̤a	ḥādis̤a.
Accidentally		ittifāḳan	ittifāḳan	nā gumān.
Account		ḥisāb	ḥisāb	ḥisāb.
Ache	xiii. 7	dard	dard	dard.
Across	ix. 16	pare	'ubūr	pore.
Active		chālāk	chābuk	chālāk.
Add to	v. 3	jama' k.	jama' k.	jama' k.
Advertisement		ishtihār	ishtihār	ishtihār.
Advice	ii. 42	ṣalāḥ	ṣalāḥ	nyat.
Adze	xi. 19	basūlā	tesha	tark͟hag.
After	v. 23	pīchhe	ba'd	wruste.
Afternoon	viii. 46	tīsre pahar	sipahar	māspek͟hīn.
Again	ii. 49	phir	bāz	bya.
Against (contrary to)				
Age		'umr	'umr	'umr.
Agent		gumāshta	gumāshta	gumāshta.

English.	*Ref.*	*Urdū.*	*Persian.*	*Pashtū.*
Agree to	ii. 56	kabūl k.	rāzī shudan	rāzī k.
Air		hawā	hawā	bād.
Alike	viii. 34	barābar	barābar	barābar.
All	ii. 66	tamām	tamām	tol
Almanac		jantrī	taḳwīn	jantraī.
Almond	iii. 16	bādām	bādām	bādām.
Alone	ix. 74	akelā	tanhā	tanhā.
Also	i. 63	bhī	ham	ham.
Always	v. 23	hamesha	hamesha	mudām.
Ambuscade		ghāt	kamīn gāh	kamīn gāh.
Ammunition		golī bārūt	golī bārūd, saranjām i jangī	golaī dārū.
Anchor		langar	langar	langar.
And	i. 9	aur	wa *or* o	au.
Angle		zāwiya	zāwiya	zāwiya.
Angry		khafa	khafa	khapa.
Animal		jānwar	jānwar	zanāwar.
Ankle	xiii. 23	takhnā	shitālang	marwand.
Anna	vi. 2	ānā	ānā	ānā.
Annoyance		diḳḳ	taḳlif	rabaṛ.
Another	viii. 60	dūsrā	dīgar	bul.
Answer	i. 61	jawāb	jawāb	dzawāb.
Antelope	i. 14	hirun	āhū	osai.
Anvil		nihāī	sandān	sandān.
Anyone	ii. 29	koī	kase	tsok.
Apart	viii. 41	alag	'alāḥida	byal.
Approve		pasand k.	manẓūr k.	pasandawal.
Apple	iii. 30	seb	seb	manre.
Apricot		zard ālū	zard ālū	zard ālū.
Arch	xi. 13	ḍāt	kamān, miḥrāb	miḥrāb.
Arithmetic		ḥisāb kitāb	siyāḳat	shumār.
Arm		hāth	bāzū	lās.
Armed	ix. 26	hathyārband	aslaḥdār	wasladār.
Army	xii. 4	fauj	fauj	fauz.
Arrange, to		ārāsta k.	ārāsta ḳ.	joṛawal.
Arrive, to	v. 22	pahūnchnā	rasīdan	rasedal.
Artillery	xii. 16	topkhāna	topkhāna	topkhāna.
Ask, to	xi. 85	pūchhnā	pursīdan	pukhtal.
Ask for, to	vi. 19	māngnā	khwāstan	ghukhtal.
Asleep	ii. 32	sotā	bakhwāb	oda.
Ashes		rākh	khākistar	īre.
Ass		gadhā	khar	khar.
Assistance		madad	madad	kumak.
At home	ii. 32	ghar meṅ	ba khāna	pa kor ke.
Attach, to	x. 6	bāndhnā	basta k.	taṛal.
Attack, to	xii. 22	ḥamla k.	ḥamla k.	halla k.
Auger	xi. 20	barma	barma	barma.
Autumn	iv. 17	sāonī	kharīf	manāī.

English.	*Ref.*	*Urdū.*	*Persian.*	*Pashtū.*
Awake	ii. 33	jāgtā	bedār	wīkh.
Awl (auger)				
Axe	xi. 18	kulhārī	tabar	tabar.
Axle	xii. 7	dhurā	mīl	dura.
Back, the		pīṭh	pusht	mlā.
Back	xi. 1	laut	wāpas	wrusto.
Bad		kharāb, bad	bad	bad.
Bag		thailī	kīsa	hamyānaī.
Bag, tent	viii. 23	shalīta	shalīta	shalīta.
Baggage	viii. 24	asbāb	asbāb	asbāb.
Bake, to		pakānā	pukhtan	pakhawal.
Baker		rotiwālā	nān paz	ḍoḍai pakhawunkai.
Bamboo	x. 2	bāṅs	nai e hindī	darwai.
Bank	viii. 42	kināra	lab	ghāṛa.
Banker	vi. 19	mahājan	sāhūkār	ṣarrāf.
Bark	i. 66	chhilkā	post	postakaī.
Barley	vi. 16	jau	jau	urbushe.
Barrel, gun	xii. 10	nāl	nal	nalaī.
Barber		nāī	ḥajjām	nāī.
Basket	xi. 43	ṭokrī	sabd	ṭokraī.
Basin		bartan	ẓarf	kālai, bartan.
Bath		ghusal	ghusl	lambal.
Batten *or* lath		bargā	barga, dastak	barge, dastakī.
Battle		laṛāī	jang	jang.
Bayonet		sangīn	sangīn	sangīn.
Bay, colour	viii. 62	lāl	kumed	kumed.
Beak		chonch	minḳār	makhūka.
Bear	ii. 114	bhālū	khirs	melū.
Beard		dārhī	rīsh	gira.
Beam	xi. 76	shāhtīr, kaṛī		shātīr.
Beat, to	i. 31	mārnā	zadan	wahal.
Beat, to, for game	viii. 74			
Become, to	i. 56	hojānā	shudan	kedal.
Bed	ii. 75	bistar	bistar	kaṭ.
Bedstead	viii. 57	chārpāī	palang	kaṭ.
Bee		madhmakhī	zanbūr i shahd	muchaī.
Before	iv. 7	pahle	pesh	wṛānde.
Begin, to	iv. 20	lagnā	shurū' k.	shurū' k.
Behind	ix. 12	pīchhe	pas	wruste.
Believe, to		mānnā, sach jānnā	bāwar k.	bāwar k.
Bell		ghantālī	jaras	gungrū.
Belly	ix. 83	pet	shikam	geḍa.
Belong, to	ix. 28			
Belt, waist	xii. 14	petī	kamar band	petaī.

English.	*Ref.*	*Urdū.*	*Persian.*	*Pashtū.*
Belt, cross	xii. 14	partalā	partala	partala.
Benefit, good	ii. 34	fāida	fāida	sūd.
Better	ix. 65	bihtar	bihtar	bihtar.
Between	x. 5	bīch meṅ	miyān	pa myanz ke.
Beyond	x. 8	pare	ān sū	pore.
Bill (account)				
Birth		paidāish	paidāish	paidāish.
Bird		chiṛiyā	murgh	margha.
Bite, to		kāṭnā	dandān zadan, gazīdan	chichal.
Bitter	iii. 22	kaṛwā	talkh	trīkh.
Black		kālā	siyāh	tor.
Blacksmith		luhār	āhangar	pash.
Blame, to		'aib lagānā	badnām k.	badnām k.
Blanket	viii. 38	kamal	shālak	sharaī.
Bleed,to(neut.)		lahū jānā	khūn rekhtan	wīne tsātsedal.
Bleed, to (act.)		rag kholnā	faṣd k.	rag wahal.
Blind		andhā	kor	ṛūnd.
Blossom, to	iv. 17	phūlnā	shiguftan	ghoṛedal.
Blood		lahū	khūn	wīne.
Blow, to (wind)	iv. 19	chalnā	wazīdan	chaledal.
Blow, a		ghūṅsā	ẓarb	sūk.
Blue		līlā	nīl, kabūd	nīlī.
Board	xi. 98	takhta	takhta	ṭakhta.
Boat	viii. 25	nāo	kishtī	beṛaī.
Body		badan	badan	tan.
Boil, to	iii. 6	josh k.	josh k.	īkhawal.
Bolt, for door		chhitkanī	darband	aṛamai.
Bolt	xi. 20	kābila	kābila	aṛamai.
Bone	iii. 23	haddī	ustukhwān	hadukai.
Bore, to	xi. 20	chhed k.	suftan	surai k.
Born		paidā	paidā	paidā.
Book	i. 17	kitāb	kitāb	kitāb.
Boot	i. 22	būṭ	moza	paṅṛe.
Both	viii. 34	donoṅ	har do	dwāṛa.
Bother, to	ii. 14	diḳḳ d.	diḳḳ k.	rabṛawal.
Bottom	ix. 42	talā	tah	talai.
Box	ii. 66	sandūḳ	sandūḳ	sandūḳ.
Boy	i. 2	laṛkā	ṭifl	halak.
Brain		godā	maghz	māghzuh.
Branch	xi. 36	tahnī	shākh	tsānga.
Bran	viii. 65	chokar	sabūs	chokar.
Brass	vi. 18	pītal	biranj	zyar.
Brave		bahādur	sherdil	zaṛāwar.
Bravery		surtā	bahādurī, jur'at	zaṛāwartya.
Bread	viii. 7	roṭī	nān	ḍoḍaī.
Breadth		chauṛāī	'arẓ	planwālai.
Break, to		toṛnā	shikastan	mātawal.

English.	*Ref.*	*Urdū.*	*Persian.*	*Pashtū.*
Breakfast	iii. 1	hāẓirī	nān i chāsht	nāshta.
Breast		chhātī	sīna	sīna.
Breath		dam	dam	dam.
Bribe		rishwat	rishwat	badye.
Brick		īnt	khisht	khukhta.
Bricklayer	i. 65	rāj	gilkār	gilkār.
Bridge	i. 24	pul	pul	pul.
Bridle	viii. 33	lagām	ḳāiza, jalo	ḳāiza.
Bring, to	i. 32	lānā	āwurdan	rāwṛal.
Brook		nahr	jū *or* ābrau	lakhtai.
Brother	i. 1	bhāī	barādar	wror.
Brush, to		jhāṛnā	takānīdan	takawal.
Bucket		bāltī	dalw	boḳa.
Bug		khatmal	khasak	kaṭmal.
Build, to	i. 48	banānā	ta'mīr k.	joṛawal.
Building	xi. 12	makān	makān	makān.
Bull		bail	nar gāo	ghwāyai.
Bullet	xii. 11	golī	golī	golaī.
Bundle	vii. 3	gathrī	basta	buḳchaī.
Burn, to	iii. 40	jalnā	sokhtan	swal.
Bush	ix. 69	jhāṛī	būta	būtai.
Business	ii. 20	kām	kār	kār.
Busy		kām par	mashghūl	mashghūl.
But	i. 10	lekin	ammā	wale.
Butcher		ḳaṣāb	ḳaṣāī	ḳaṣāb.
Butter	iii. 14	makhan	maska	kuch.
Button		batan	tukma	tukma.
Buttress		pushta	pushta	pushtaī.
Buy, to	i. 36	mol lenā	kharīdan	ākhastal.
By		se	az	la...na.
Cage		pinjrā	ḳafaṣ	panjra.
Calamity		āfat	āfat	āfat.
Calculation		ḥisāb	shumār	shmār.
Call, to	ii. 13	bulānā	ṭalbīdan	balal.
Camel	vi. 14	ūnṭ	shutur	ūkh.
Camp (halting-place)	i. 69			
Can (able)				
Canal		nahr	nahr	lakhtai.
Candle	ii. 10	battī	ḳandīl	baṭai.
Cannon		top	top	top.
Cautery	xiii. 18	dāgh	dāgh	dāgh.
Cap, for head		ṭopī	kulāh	ṭopai.
Cap, for gun		ṭopī	patākhī e bandūḳ	paṭākhe.
Caravan	xii. 22	ḳāfila	ḳāfila	kārwān.
Careful	ii. 3	khabardār	hoshyār	bedār.

English.	*Ref.*	*Urdū.*	*Persian.*	*Pashtū.*
Careless (negligent)				
Carpenter		baṛhāī	najjār	tarkāṅṛ.
Carpet	ii. 113	farsh	farsh	farsh.
Carrot		gājar	zardak	gājare.
Carry, to	x. 23	lejānā	burdan	wṛal.
Cart	xi. 72	gāṛhī	'araba	gaḍai.
Cartridge	xii. 13	kārtūs	kārtūs, wuzun	kārtūs.
Cash	ii. 27	naḳd	naḳd	rok.
Cask		pīpā	khum i chobī	pīpā.
Cast iron			chūan	
Cast, to	xii. 11			
Cat		billī	gurba	pīsho.
Catch, to	ii. 110	pakaṛnā	giriftan	nīwal.
Cattle	viii. 31	jānwar	maweshī	dangar.
Centre	xi. 14	markaz	markaz	manz.
Ceiling	xi. 87	chhat	saḳf	chat.
Chain	x. 21	zanjīr	zanjīr	zanzīr.
Chair	ii. 24	kursī	kursī	tsaukai.
Chamber, of gun		koṭhī	khazāna	khazāna.
Change, to		badal k.	badal k.	badlawal.
Change money, to	vi. 8	ṭoṛānā	khurda k.	mātawal.
Channel	ix. 80	nālā	shākh i jū	wela.
Chapter	vii. 9	bāb	bāb	bāb.
Charge, to	xii. 19	ḍhāwā k.	ḥamla k.	halla k.
Charcoal	iii. 39	koelā	zughāl	skāra.
Chatter, to	ii. 50	baknā	harzagoī k.	behūda wayal.
Cheap	vi. 7	sastā	arzān	arzān.
Cheese	iii. 24	panīr	panīr	panīr.
Cheque	vi. 19	hunḍwī	kāghaz	hundaī.
Cherry		shāh ālū	shāh ālū	shāh ālū.
Chess		shatranj	shatranj	shatranj.
Chessman		goṭā	nard	nard.
Chessboard		bisāṭ	bisāṭ	shatranj.
Child	v. 21	bachcha	ṭifl	halak.
Chimney		angīṭhī	bukhārī	angītaī.
Chief	ix. 45	sardār	sardār	malak.
Chisel	xi. 81	rukhānī	iskana	tswarlai.
Circle		dāira	dāira	dāira.
City	i. 25	shahr	shahr	kkhahr.
Civil, service		mulkī	mulkī *or* ahl i ḳalam	mulkī.
Claim		da'wa	da'wa	da'wa.
Claw		panja	changal	panja.
Clay	xi. 38	chiknī mittī	gil i charb	zīga khāwra.
Clean	i. 49	ṣāf	ṣāf	pāk.

English.	*Ref.*	*Urdū.*	*Persian.*	*Pashtū.*
Climate	iv. 18	āb o hawā	āb o hawā	hawā.
Cloak		bārān koṭ	chog͟ha, bālā-posh, labāda	chog͟ha.
Clock		ghanṭā	sā 'at	ganṭā.
Close	xi. 34	nazdīk	mutaṣṣil	nizhde.
Cloth	i. 13	kapṛā	pārcha	k͟hamtā.
Cloth seller	i. 68	kapṛe wālā	bazzāz	bazāz.
Clothes	i. 50	kapṛe	poshāk	jāme.
Cloud	iv. 14	bādal	abr	wryadz.
Coarse		moṭā	luk	g͟hat.
Coat	i. 41	kuṛtā	farg͟hal, jāma	k͟halka.
Cocoa-nut		nāryal	nājīl	garaī
Cock, of gun		ghoṛā	kulang	chirg, kulang.
Cock, fowl		murg͟h	murg͟h	chirg.
Coffee	iii. 11	kāfī	ḳahwā	ḳahwa.
Cold		ṭhanḍā	sard	soṛ.
Cold weather	iv. 2	jāṛā	sarma	zhamai.
Cold, illness	xiii. 17	ẓukām	ẓukām	sāṛa.
Collect, to	ix. 56	jama' k.	jama' k.	ṭolawal.
Colour	ii. 98	rang	rang	rang.
Comb		kanghī	shāna	gumandz.
Come, to	ii. 1	ānā	āmadam	rātlal.
Command	ii. 58	ḥukm	ḥukm	ḥukm.
Commencement	xiii. 6	ibtidā	ibtidā	shurū'.
Common		'ām	'ām.	'ām.
Comparison		nisbat	tashbīh	nisbat.
Compass	x. 7	kampās	kampās	kampās.
Compasses, pair of	xi. 96	parkār	parkār	parkār.
Complainant		mudda'ī	mudda'ī	mudda'ī.
Complete		pūrā	tamām	pūra.
Condition, a	xi. 3	sharṭ	sharṭ	sharṭ.
Conform, to	xi. 50	muwāfiḳ k.	muwāfiḳ k.	barābar k.
Consent(agree)				
Consequence	ii. 77	muẓāyaḳa	muẓāyaḳa	k͟habara.
Constipation	xiii. 16	ḳabẓ	ḳabẓ	ḳabẓ.
Contract		ṭhekā	ijāra	ijāra.
Contractor		ṭhekadār	ijāradār	ijāradār.
Contrary to		k͟hilāf	k͟hilāf, bar 'aks	khilāf.
Contented		rāẓī	rāẓī	rāẓī.
Cook, to	iii. 23	pakānā	pukhtān	pak͟hawal.
Cook	ii. 13	bāwarchī	bāwarchī	ḍoḍai pak͟hwunkai.
Cool	iii. 19	ṭhanḍā	k͟hunak	soṛ.
Coolie	ii. 71	ḳulī	ḳulī	mazdūr.
Copper	vi. 17	tānbā	mis	mis.
Cord	x. 6	ḍorī	respāṅ	mazai.

English.	Ref.	Urdū.	Persian.	Pashtū.
Corn	viii. 8	dāna	dāna	dāna.
Corner	xi. 11	konā	gosha	kunj.
Corporal	xii. 24	nāik	nāik	nāik.
Correct	xi. 11	ṭhīk	durust	jukht.
Cotton		rūī	punba	punba, mālūch.
Cough	xiii. 15	khāṅsī	sulfa	tūkhai.
Country		mulk	mulk	mulk.
Court, royal		sabhā	dargāh	darbār.
Court, judge's		kachahrī	dār ul 'adālat	kacharaī.
Cow	i. 12	gāī	gāo	ghwā.
Cow-dung wash	xi. 94	gobarī	sirgīn i gāo	gobar.
Cow-dung	iii. 32	uplā	sirgīn i gāo	ghushāya.
Crack	xi. 83	darz	darz	darz.
Cream	iii. 12	malāī	ḳaimāgh	perawai.
Creditor	vi. 22	ḳarz khwāh	ḳarz khwāh	porawurai.
Crime		gunāh	gunāh	gunāh
Crooked		ṭeṛhā	kaj	kog
Cross out, to		ḳalam khīnchnā	ḳalam kashīdan	ḳalam nākhkal
Crowbar		gadālā		
Cubit (1½ feet)		hāth	dast	lās.
Cup	iii. 9	piyāla	piyāla, finjān	piyāla.
Current		bahāo	jiriyān	terawalai.
Cut, to	i. 47	kāṭnā	burīdan	prekawal.
Dagger	ix. 27	chhurā	peshḳabẓ	chāṛa.
Dāl	ix. 52	mūng, dāl	māsh	dāl.
Damage	xi. 73	nuḳṣān	nuḳṣan	nuḳṣān.
Damp	iii. 40	gīlā	tar	lūnd.
Danger	ix. 73	dahohat	khaṭra	ḍar.
Dangerously wounded	xii. 25	kārī zakhmī	kārī zakhmī	sakht zhobal.
Dark		andherā	tārīk	tārīk
Dark blue		gahrā nīlā	tīragūn nīl	tor rang nīl.
Date		khajūr	khurmā	khajūra.
Daughter		beṭī	dukhtar	lūr.
Day	ii. 71	din	roz	wradz.
Day before yesterday	v. 26	parsoṅ	parī roz	bul parūn.
Day after to-morrow	v. 26	parsoṅ	pas i farda	bal-sabā.
Dead		mūā	murda	marai, mar
Deaf		bahrā	kar	kūṅṛ.
Dear		piyāra	'azīz	'aziz.
Dear (in price)	vi. 7	mahngā	girān	grān.
Death		maut	maut	marg.
Debtor	vi. 23	ḳarẓdār	ḳarẓdār	porawuṛai.

English.	*Ref.*	*Urdū.*	*Persian.*	*Pashtū.*
Defeat	xii. 26	shikast	shikast	mātī.
Defendant		mudda'ā 'alaihi	mudda'ā 'alaihi	mudda' ā 'alaihi
Degrees of lon. & lat.		ṭūl o 'arz ke darje	darjahā e ṭūl o 'arz	darjahā e ṭūl o 'arz.
Delay	viii. 55	der	tā<u>kh</u>ir	dīl.
Depth		gahrāī	'umuḳ	zhawarwālai.
Descend		utarnā	faro raftan	kuzedal.
Desert, a		jangal	ṣaḥrā	maira.
Desire, to		chāhnā	<u>kh</u>wāstan	<u>gh</u>u<u>kh</u>tal.
Dew	iv. 16	os	shabnam	par<u>kh</u>a.
Diagonal		munhanī	munhanī	munhanī.
Diamond		hīrā	almās	almās.
Diarrhœa	xiii. 10	dast	shikam rau	da gede bahedal.
Die, to	viii. 60	marnā	murdan	mṛal.
Difference		faraḳ	tafāwut	farḳ.
Difficult	ii. 99	mushkil	mushkil	grān.
Dig, to	xi. 25	khodnā	kandan	kandal.
Dinner	iii. 2	khānā	tu'ām nān	ḍoḍaī.
Direction	ix. 1	ṭaraf	sū	<u>kh</u>wā.
Dirty	xii. 7	mailā	chirkīn	<u>kh</u>īran.
Disease	xiii. 4	bīmārī	maraẓ	bīmārī.
Dish	iii. 10	rikābī	ḳāb	tālai.
Dislocated, to be	xiii. 24	utar jānā	barāmadan	<u>kh</u>atal.
Dismount, to,	viii. 3	utarnā	pāyān shudan	kuzedal.
Disowning, a son		'āḳ	'āḳ	'āḳ.
Distance	x. 12	fāṣila	fāṣila	wut.
Distinctly	ix. 32	ṣaḥīḥ	ṣaḥīḥ	ṣaḥiḥ.
District	iv. 5	'ilāḳa	ẓilla'	'ilāḳa.
Distribute, to	viii. 48	bānṭnā	taḳsīm k.	weshal.
Divide, to (distribute)				
Division		taḳsīm	taḳsīm	wesh.
Divorce		ṭalāḳ	ṭilāḳ	ṭalāḳ.
Doctor		ḥakīm	ḥakīm	ṭabīb.
Dog	ii. 93	kutta	sag	spai.
Door	ii. 8	darwāza	darwāza	war.
Door bar		musabbar	darband	
Double		dochand	dochand	dwāzala.
Down	ii. 11	nīche	pāyān	kūz.
Drag, to	x. 23	khīnchnā	kashīdan	tskawal.
Drain		morī, nalī	ābrau *or* jū	la<u>kh</u>tai.
Draw, to (plans)	vii. 4	banānā	kashīdan	k<u>kh</u>kul.
Drawers		pāe jāma	pāe jāma	parṭūg.

English.	*Ref.*	*Urdū.*	*Persian.*	*Pashtū.*
Drawing, a		naksha	naḳsha	naḳsha.
Dreadful		darāonī	hāil	khaufnāk.
Dream, a		sapnā	khwāb	khob.
Drill, military		ḳawā'id	ḳawā'id	ḳawā'id.
Drink, to	i. 33	pīnā	noshīdan, khūrdan	tskal.
Drive, to (game)	viii. 73	hānkā lānā	rāndan	rā āṛawal.
Droop, to	xi. 36	lataknā	āwekhtan	zwaṛand kedal.
Druggist		pansārī	dārū farosh	pasārī.
Drum	xii. 28	dol	duhal	dol.
Dry	i. 50	sūkhā	khushk	wuch.
Duck		baṭak	baṭ	baṭa.
Dumb		gūngā	lāl	gung.
Duty	xii. 25	naukrī	naukrī	naukarī.
Dwell, to (live)	i. 23			
Dyer		rangrez	rangrez	dobī.
Each	v. 15	har ek	har yak	har yau.
Ear		kān	gosh	ghwag.
Earlier	ii. 60	āge	peshtar	wṛānde
Early	ii. 82	baṛī fajr	'ala-ul-ṣabāh	ṣabāī wakhti.
Earth	xi. 44	miṭṭī	gil	khāwra.
Easy		āsān	āsān	āsān.
Easily		āsānī se	ba āsānī	pa āsāntiya sara.
East	ix. 78	pūrab	mashriḳ	nmar khāta.
Eat, to	i. 34	khānā	khurdan	khwaṛal.
Eaves spout		parnālā	ābrau	parnāla.
Eclipse of sun	v. 26	sūraj gahan	kusūf	da nmar tandar
Eclipse of moon		chandragrahan	khusūf	da myāshte tandar.
Edge	viii. 2	kināra	lab, kināra	ghāṛa.
Edge (of a tool)		dhār	kināra	ghāṛa.
Education	vii. 17	ta'līm	ta'līm	tarbīyat.
Egg	iii. 6	andā	tukhm	oya *or* hā.
Elbow		kuhnī	mirfaḳ	marwand.
Elephant	i. 9	hāthī	fīl	hātī.
Embroidered, with gold		ṭila bāfta	muraṣṣa', zar-dokhta	ṭiladār.
Empty	ii. 66	khālī	khālī	tash.
End	v. 20	ākhir	ākhir	
Enemy	xii. 19	dushman	ḥasūd	dukhman.
Enlist, to	xii. 2	bhartī k.	muḳarrar k.	naukarawal.
Enough		bas	kāfī	bas.
Enquire, to	xi. 72	pūchhnā	daryāft k.	pukhtana k.
Entertainment		ẓiyāfat	ẓiyāfat	milmastyā.
Equal		barābar	yaksān	barābar.

English.	*Ref.*	*Urdū.*	*Persian.*	*Pashtū.*
Escape		bachāo	rihāī	bach.
Estimate		taḵẖmīna, istimaṭ	taḵẖmīnīḳīmat	taḵẖmīnī ḳimat.
Even (*adv.*)		bhī	ham	ham.
Evening	iv. 3	shām	shām	māḵẖām.
Exactly	viii. 47	ṭhīk	'ain	barābar.
Examine, to	v. 25	mulāḥaẓa k.	mulāḥaẓa k.	katal.
Excavation	xi. 74	khodāī	ḵẖandaḳ	kandana.
Excellent	xi. 52	bihtar	ḵẖūb	ḵẖuh.
Extinguish, to, put out		bujhānā	gul k.	maṛawal.
Extreme		āḵẖirī	āḵẖirī	wrustanai.
Eye	x. 4	āṅkh	chashm	starga.
Eyebrow		bhaweṅ	ābrū	barwaṭe.
Face		muṅh	rū	maḵẖ.
Fair	i. 51	gorā	sufed	spīn.
Fall, to		girnā	uftādan	prewatal.
Fall into, to		milnā	raftan	gaḍedal.
False	ix. 89	jhūṭh	darogh	darogh.
Family	ii. 48	kutumb	ḳabīla	ṭabar.
Famine	ii. 54	kāl	ḳaḥṭ	ḳaḥṭ.
Fan (punkha)				
Far (distance)				
Fare (hire)				
Farrier		na'lband	na'lband	na'lband.
Fast	viii. 49	jald	zūd	gaṛandai.
Fat	ix. 21	charbī	charbī	wāzda.
Fate	iii. 31	ḳismat	ḳismat	naṣīb.
Father		bāp	padar	plār.
Fault	i. 4	ḳuṣūr	gunāh	ḳuṣūr.
Fear		ḍar	ḵẖauf	wyara.
Fear, to	ix. 74	ḍarnā	tarsīdan	wyaredal.
Feed, to (act.)	ii. 69	khilānā	ḵẖurānīdan	ḵẖurawal.
Feed, to, as birds	viii. 75	chugna	charīdan	tsaredal.
Fever	xiii. 3	bukhār	tap	taba.
Few		thoṛā	chand	lag.
Field	i. 4	khet	kisht	kaṭai.
Fig	iii. 20	anjīr	anjīr	īndzar.
File	viii. 54	retī	sūhān	sūhān.
Fill, to	vi. 26	bhar denā	pur k.	dakawal.
Find, to	vii. 12	pānā	yāftan	mundal.
Fine, a	ii. 3	jurīmāna	jurīmāna	tāwān.
Fine	ii. 101	mahīn	bārīk	bārīk.
Finish, to	v. 23	tamām k.	tamām k.	pūra k.
Fire		āg	ātish	or.
Fireplace		angīṭhī	ātish ḵẖāna	ngharai.

English.	*Ref.*	*Urdū.*	*Persian.*	*Pashtū.*
Fire, to	i. 64	chalāṇā	sar kardan	chalawal.
Firewood (wood)		lakṛī	hezam	largī.
First	vii. 9	pahlā	awwal	wṛambai.
Fish	iii. 17	machhlī	māhī	kab.
Fit, to	viii. 51	biṭhānā	durust k.	lagawal.
Flag	x. 4	jhanḍī	bairaḳ	janḍā.
Flat	xi. 62	hamwār	hamwār	barābar.
Flame		bhabūkā	shu'la	shu'la.
Flash		chamak	shu'la	shu'la.
Flea		pisū	kaik	wraga.
Flee, to	xii. 23	bhāgnā	gurekhtan	takhtedal.
Flesh (meat)				
Flint		chaḳmaḳ	chaḳmāḳ	bakar.
Flood	xi. 73	sailāb	sailāb	nīz.
Floor	xi. 80	farsh	farsh	farsh.
Flour	ix. 49	āṭā	ārd	oṛuh.
Flow, to	ix. 63	bahnā	raftan, jārī sh.	bahidal.
Flower	i. 54	phūl	gul	gul.
Flurry, to	viii. 28	ghabrānā	tarsānīdan	darawal.
Fly, to		uṛnā	parīdan	ālwatal.
Fly, a		makhī	magas	much.
Fog	v. 26	kuhāsā	bukhār, kusūf	dūnd.
Food		khānā	khoṛāk	khurāk.
Foolish	ii. 107	bewuḳūf	aḥmaḳ	aḥmaḳ.
Foot	i. 60	pāṅw	pā	pkhā.
Foot, on		paidal	piyāda	piyāda.
Forage		chāra	chāra	wākhuh au dāna.
Force		zabardastī	zabardastī	zorāwarī.
Fore	viii. 53	aglā	peshīn	rāndīnai.
Forehead	xiii. 1	mātha	peshānī	tandai.
Fork		kāṅṭā	changāl, do shākha	do kkhākkha.
Forest	ix. 19	jangal	jaṅgal, besha	dzangal.
Forget, to	ii. 4	bhūlnā	farāmosh k.	herawal.
Forgiven		mu'āf	mu'āf	mu'āf.
Formerly	i. 68	peshtar	peshtar	wṛānde.
Fort	ii. 16	ḳil'a	ḳil'a	ḳil'a.
Forward	ii. 81	āge	pesh	wṛānde.
Foundation	xi. 5	bunyād	bunyād	wekh.
Fowl	iii. 36	murghī	māḳiyān	chirga.
Fox	i. 64	lomṛī	robāh	soya.
Frequently	iv. 4	akṣar	akṣar	akṣar.
Fresh	iii. 7	tāza	tāza	tāza.
Friend		dost	dost	yār.
Frightened, to be	viii. 29	darnā	tarsīdan	daredal.
Frog, of foot	viii. 51	putlī	miyān i sum	putlai.

English.	*Ref.*	*Urdū.*	*Persian.*	*Pashtū.*
Front, in	ix. 23	āge	pesh	wṛānde.
Freeze, to	iv. 5	jam jānā	yakh bastan	kangal kedal.
Fruit	iv. 17	phal	mewa	mewa.
Full		bhar	pur	ḍak.
Full, in	xi. 2	kull	bebāḳ	pūrā.
Gallop, to (trans.)	ix. 40	dauṛānā	doānīdan	zghalawal.
Game		shikār	ṣaid	shikār.
Garden	ii. 112	baghīcha	bāgh	bāghcha.
Gardener		mālī	bāghbān	mālī.
Garlic		thūn	sīr	yage, ūgā.
Gelding	viii. 62	akhta	akhta	khasī.
Generally	vi. 14	akṣar	akṣar	akṣar.
Geometry		'ilm i masāhat	'ilm i masāhat	kach.
Get, to		hāṣil k.	yāftan	mundal.
Ginger		sonṭh	adrak	adrak.
Girl		laṛkī	dukhtar	woṛkī.
Girth	viii. 32	tang	tang	tang.
Give, to	i. 18	denā	dādan	warkawal.
Ghee	vi. 15	ghī	raughan i zard	ghwarī.
Glad		khush	khush	khwakh.
Glass		shīsha	shīsha	shīsha.
Glove		dastāna	dastāna	dastāna.
Goat	i. 35	bakrī	buz	wzah.
Go, to	i. 44	jānā	raftan	tlal.
Goldsmith		sunār	zargar	zargar.
Gold		sonā	zar	sru zar.
Gold mohr	vi. 1	ashrafī	ashrafī	butkaī.
Gong	v. 25	ghanṭā	jaras (a bell)	ganṭā.
Good		achchhā	khūb	khuh.
Goods	vi. 23	asbāb	asbāb	māl.
Goose		rājhāṅs	ḳāz	loya baṭa.
Government		sarkār	sarkār	sarkār.
Grain	vi. 7	ghalla	ghalla	ghala.
Gram	viii. 65	channā	nākhūd	chaṅṛe.
Grandfather, *p.*	i. 7	dādā	jad i padarī	nikuh.
" *m.*		nānā	jad i mādarī	nānā.
Grandmother *p.*		dādī	mādar i padar	nyā.
" *m.*		nānī	mādar i mādar	nānaī.
Grape	iii. 20	angūr	tāk	angūr.
Grass	viii. 8	ghās	kāh, gyāh	wākhuh.
Great	ii. 100	baṛā	buzurg	loe.
Green	iii. 30	hārā	sabz	shuwa
Groom	ii. 13	sāīs	sāīs	sāīs.
Ground	ii. 83	zamīn	zamīn	zmuka
Guard	xii. 6	gārḍ	ṭilāya	gārat.

English.	*Ref.*	*Urdū.*	*Persian.*	*Pashtū.*
Guest		mihmān	mihmān	mihmān
Guide		rastā batāne wālā	rāh numā, badraḳa	lār khayunkai.
Gun	i. 42	bandūḳ	tufang	ṭupak.
Gun, cannon	xii. 17	top	top	top.
Gunpowder	xii. 16	bārūt	bārūd	dārū.
Hail	iv. 11	olā	zhālā	zhālaī.
Hair		bāl	mū	wekhtuh.
Half	v. 5	ādhā	nīm, niṣf	nīm.
Halter	viii. 39	agārī	kamand-i-pesh	tarsarai.
Halting place	viii. 55	parāo	manzīl	manzil.
Hammer		mārtol	chakush, puchak	tsatak.
Hammer of gun (cock)	xii. 7			
Hand	i. 27	hāth	dast	lās.
Handle	xi. 29	dasta	dasta	lāstai.
Handkerchief		rūmāl	rūmāl	rūmāl.
Handsome	i. 10	khūbṣūrat	khūbrū	kkhayasta.
Hang, to (act.)	ii. 86	latkānā	āwezānīdan	zwaṛand k.
Hard	...	sakht	sakht	sakht.
Hare	i. 39	khargosh	khargosh	soya.
Harness	viii. 44	sāz	sāz o sāmān	da ās asbāb.
Harvest	iv. 13	faṣl	faṣl	faṣal.
Haste	ii. 6	jaldī	zūdī	zir.
Hat	i. 18	topī	kulāh	topai.
Have, to	i. 28	rakhnā	dāshtan	laral.
Head	i. 26	sir	sar	sar.
Headache	xiii. 7	dard i sar	dard i sar	dard i sar.
Headstall		nukta	nukta	sardawāl.
Heal, to (neut.)		changā honā	jor shudan	joredal.
Health		mizāj	mizāj	mizāj.
Heap		ḍher	toda	ḍerai.
Hear, to	i. 61	sunnā	shunīdan	auredal.
Heart		dil	dil	zruh.
Heat (hot season)	iv. 1			
Heavy		bhārī	sangīn	drūnd.
He	i. 23	wuh	o	hagha.
Heel		eṛī	ka'b, pai, 'aḳab	pūnda.
Heel ropes	viii. 40	pichhāṛī	rasanhāe pasīn	pichārai.
Height		ūnchāī	bulandī	uchatwālai.
Heir		wāriṣ	wāriṣ	wariṣ.
Hemp	xi. 9	san	san	saṅṛ.
Her	i. 10	us-kā(-ke, -kī)	-i -o *or* -ash	da haghe.
Here	xi. 40	yahāṅ	īnjā	dalta.
Height		ūnchāī	bulandī	uchatwālai.

English.	*Ref.*	*Urdū.*	*Persian.*	*Pashtū.*
Hill	viii. 1	pahāṛ	koh	ghar.
Hills, the	iv. 21	pahāṛ	kohistān	ghrūna.
Him	i. 61	us ko	o *or* ash	hagha.
Hind	viii. 53	pichhlā	pasīn	wrustanai.
Hindrance		roktok	insidād	muzāḥamat.
Hinge		ḳabza	ḳabza, chap-rās, H.	ḳabza.
Hip		khūtaṛ	surīn	kunaṭai.
Hire	viii. 36	karāya	karāya	kirāya.
His	i. 6	us-kā (-ke, -kī)	-i -o *or* -ash	da hagha.
History	vii. 16	tārīkh	tawārīkh	tārīkh.
Hither	ii. 1	idhar	īnjā, īnsū	dale.
Hold, to		thānbnā	giriftan	nīwal.
Hole	i. 67	chhed	surākh	sūṛai.
Hollow				
Home, at	ii. 32	ghar meṅ	ba khāna	ha kor ke.
Hook		kunḍā	kināra	kunḍā.
Hook, fish-		kunḍī	ḳulāb	kunḍaī.
Horn		singh	shākh	shkar.
Horse	i. 9	ghoṛā	asp	ās.
Horse-shoe		na'l	na'l	na'l.
Hospital		āspitāl	dār-ul-shafā	shafā khāna.
Host		mihmāndār	mezbān	mihmān.
Hot	iii. 5	garm	garm	garma.
Hot weather	iv. 1	garmī	garmī	oṛai.
Hour	v. 10	ghanṭā	sā'at	ganṭā.
House	i. 3	ghar	khāna	kor.
How		kisṭaraḥ	chiṭaur	tsaringa.
How many	i. 20	kitnā	chand	tsomra.
Hungry	i. 59	bhūkhā	gurisna	wugai.
Hunt, to		shikār khelnā	shikār k.	kkhkār k.
Hunter (man)		shikārī	shikārī	kkhkārī.
Hurt, to	xiii. 13			
Hyena		lakaṛ baghā	kaftār	kaftār.
I	i. 30	maiṅ	man	zuh.
Ice		barf	yakh	kangal.
Idle (lazy)				
Idol		but	but	but
If	i. 56	jo	agar	ka
Ignorant	vii. 18	nādān	nādān	be 'aḳl
Ill	xiii. 5	bīmār	bīmār	najoṛ
Imagination		khiyāl	wahm	wahm.
Immediately		jhaṭpaṭ	fauran	sanī da lāsa.
Important		ahamm	ahamm	loe ẓarūrī.
Impudent		shokh	gustākh	be adab.
In	i. 21	meṅ	dar *and* ba	kkhe *or* ke.
Included	ix. 47	shāmil	shāmil	shāmil.

English.	*Ref.*	*Urdū.*	*Persian.*	*Pashtū.*
Indian corn	ix. 51	jawār	jawār	juwār.
Indigestion	xiii. 20	bad haẓmi	bad haẓmī	bad haẓmī.
Indigo		nīl	nīl	nīl.
Index	vii. 15	fihrist	fihrist	fihrist.
Indus	ix. 89	daryā e aṭak	abbā sīn	abasīn.
Industrious		miḥnatī	tandih	miḥnatī.
Influence, interest		wasīla	zarī'a	madad.
Information (news)				
Ink	vii. 1	siyāhī	roshnī	mashwāṅraī.
Inspect, to (examine)				
Insect		kīrā	kirm	chinjai.
Inside	xii. 19	bhītar	darūn	da nana.
Instead	iii. 30	bajāe	ba jāe	pa zai.
Intend, to	ii. 114	irāda rakhnā	irāda k.	nyat k.
Intention	ii. 41	irāda	irāda	nyat.
Intelligent	ii. 85	hoshyār	zīrak	hokhiyār.
Interest	vi. 24	sūd	sūd	sūd.
Interval		fāṣila	fāṣila	wut.
Intoxicated		matwālā	makhmūr	sarmast.
Invention		ījād	ījād	ījād.
Invitation		da'wat	da'wat	da'wat.
Iron	xi. 22	lohā	āhan	ospana.
Irrigation		sīṅchā sichaī	ābyārī	ābdihī
Is	i. 1	hai	ast	dai.
Island	ix. 80	tāpū	jazīra	bela.
Ivory		hāthī dānṭ	dandān i fil	da hātī ghākh
Jam	iii. 14	murabbā	murabbā	murabbā.
Jewel		jauhar	jauhar	jauhar.
Join, to		joṛnā	paiwastan	lagawal.
Joint	xi. 16	joṛ	darz	darz.
Joke, a		ṭhaṭhā, bāzī	mazākh	ṭoka.
Journey	viii. 47	safar	safar	safar.
Joyful (glad)				
Juice		'araḳ	shīra, āb	lu'āb.
Jump, to	viii. 26	kūdnā	parīdan	ṭop wahal.
Justice		inṣāf	inṣāf	inṣāf.
Key	ii. 67	kunjī	kalīd	kunjī.
Keep, to	i. 29	rakhnā	dāshtan	laral.
Kick, to	viii. 44	lāt mārnā	lakad zadan	lagata wahal.
Kid	iii. 37	bakrī kā bachcha	buz ghāla	wuz kūrai.
Kill	i. 39	mār dālnā	kushtan	wazhal.
Kiln	xi. 56	bhattī	pazāwa	baṭaī.

English.	*Ref.*	*Urdū.*	*Persian.*	*Pashtū.*
Kind		ḳism	raḳm	ḳism.
Kind (adj.)		mihrbān	mihrbān	mihrbān.
Kindness		mihrbānī	mihrbānī	mihrbānī.
King	i. 71	pādshāh	bādshāh	bādshāh.
Kink	x. 24	girih	girih	ganḍa.
Kiss, to	i. 76	chūmnā	bosīdan	kkhkwalawul.
Knave (scoundrel)				
Knee	ix. 82	guṭhnī	zānū	panḍaī.
Knife		chhurī	kārd	chāṛuh.
Know, to	ii. 40	jānnā	dānistan	pohedal.
Knowledge	vii. 18	'ilm	'ilm	'ilm.
Labour		miḥnat	miḥnat	miḥnat.
Labourer (cooly)				
Ladder	xi. 12	sīṛhī	nardbān, zīna	andarpāya.
Ladle		baṛā chamcha	kafgīr	tsamtsa.
Lady	ii. 112	mem ṣāhib	bībī ×	bībī.
Lake		tālāo	tālāb	tālāw.
Lamb	iii. 17	ḥalwān	barra	psuh.
Lame		langṛā	lang	guḍ.
Lamp	ii. 9	chirāgh	chirāgh	ḍīwā.
Lance	xii. 15	barcha	neza	naiza.
Land		zamīn	zamīm	zmuka.
Language		zabān	zabān	zhaba.
Large		baṛā	kalān	loe,
Last year		pār sāl	sāl i guzashta	paros kāl.
Late (adv.)		awere	nā waḳt	nā wakht.
Late (delay)				
Laugh, to	ii. 107	hāṅsnā	khandīdan	khandal.
Laugh at, to		khilī k.	rīsh khandī k.	ṭoke k.
Law		shar'a	shar'a	shar'a.
Lay, to, as bricks	xi. 10	lagānā	chaspānīdan	lagawal.
Layer	xi. 61	raddā	tah	tau.
Lazy	ii. 104	sust	kāhil	sust.
Lead	xii. 11	sīsā	surb	sika.
Leaf, of tree		pattī	barg	pānrī.
Leaf, of book		waraḳ	waraḳ	pāṅṛī.
Lean		dublā	lāghir	ḍangar.
Learn, to		sīkhnā	āmokhtan	zda k.
Leather		chamṛā	charm	tsarman.
Leave go, to	viii. 33	chhoṛnā	guẓāshtan	pregdal.
Left	ii. 12	bāeṅ	chap	guts.
Leg (foot)				
Leisure	ii. 17	furṣat	furṣat	wuzgārtya.
Lemon		nimbū	līmūn	nimbū.

English.	*Ref.*	*Urdū.*	*Persian.*	*Pashtū.*
Lemon-juice	iii. 13	nimbū kā 'araḳ	āb i līmū	da nimbū 'arak
Lend, to	vi. 25	ḳarẓ denā	karz dādan	por warkawai.
Let alone, to	ii. 7	rahne denā	guzāshtan	pre**kh**al.
Letter	vii. 1	chiṭṭhī	**kh**aṭṭ	**kh**aṭ.
Level	xi. 15	hamwār	hamwār	barābar.
Lid	xi. 99	ḍhakhnā	ta**kh**ta i bālā sar posh	da pās ta**kh**ta bar**gh**olai.
Lie, to	ii. 24	leṭna	darāz shudan	tsumlāstal.
Lie (false)				
Lift, to		uṭhānā	bar dāshtan	purta kawal.
Light, not dark		roshan	roshan	rok**kh**ān.
Light, to	ii. 9	jalānā	afro**kh**tan	bala k.
Light, not heavy		halkā	subuk	spuk.
Lighten, to	iv. 20			
Lightning		bijlī	barḳ	tandar.
Like, to	iii. 20	pasand k.	pasand k.	**kh**wa**kh**awal.
Limbs	xiii. 8	a'ẓā	a'zā	andāmūna.
Lime	xi. 5	chūnā	āhak	chūna.
Lime, quick		ḍallā chūuā	āhak i jāndār	zhwandaī chūna.
Lining		astar	astar	astar
Lip		honṭh	lab	shūnḍa, lab.
List		fihrist	fihrist	fihrist
Litter	xi. 66	kūṛā	**kh**ās o **kh**āshāk	**kh**as o **kh**āshāk
Little, a	ii. 88	ẕarra	ḳadare	lag *or* lug.
Live, to, ḍwell	i. 23	rahnā	māndan	osedal.
Liver	xiii. 2	jigar	jigar	dzīgar.
Lizard		chhipkalī	chilpāsa	tsarmuk**kh**ka.
Load	viii. 48	bojh	bār	bār.
Load, to, a cart	viii. 23	lādnā	bār k.	bārawal.
Load, to, a gun	xii. 20	bharnā	pur k.	dakawal.
Loan	vi. 22	ḳarẓ	ḳarẓ	por.
Lock	ii. 67	tālā	ḳufl	jandrā.
Lock, of gun		chānp	chaḳmāḳ	cha**kh**ma**kh**
Long	ii. 102	lanbā	darāz	plan.
Look for, to	viii. 59	talāsh k.	talāsh k.	laṭawal.
Loophole	xii. 29	randā	tīrkash	morcha.
Loss (damage)				
Loose	viii. 30	dhīlā	narm	narma.
Low		nīchā	faro, pāīn	lānde.
Louḍly	ii. 49	zor se	ba āwāz i buland	pa zor.
Lucerne	ix. 52	shaftal	shaftal	shantala.
Mad		pāgal	dīwāna	lewanai.
Magnifying [glass		**kh**urd bīn	**kh**urd bīn	**kh**urd bīn

English.	*Ref.*	*Urdū.*	*Persian.*	*Pashtū.*
Make, to		banānā	sākhtan	joṛawal.
Mallet	viii. 22	mallaṭ	mekhkob	ḍabalai.
Malleable	xi. 22	suchchī pattī kā	kuft pazīr	narma.
Man	i. 1	ādmī	mardum	saṛai.
Mango		ām	amba	amb.
Manner	x. 11	ṭaraḥ	ṭaur	shāṅ.
Manure	xi. 66	khāt	khāshāk	sura.
Many		bahut	bisyār	ḍer.
March, to	xii. 18	kūnch k.	kūch k.	rawāna k.
Mare	viii. 61	ghoṛī	mādiyān	āspa.
Mark	x. 3	nishān	nishān	nakha.
Market		bāzār	bāzār	bāzār.
Marriage		shādī	shādī	wāduh.
Marsh	viii. 67	jhīl	chaman, gilāb	jīl.
Master	ii. 32	ṣāḥib	ṣāḥib	ṣāḥab.
Mast		mastūl	tīr i jahāz	da jahāz tīr.
Mathematics	vii. 17	'ilm i riyāẓī	'ilm i riyāẓī	'ilm i riyāẓ.
Matting	xi. 84	chaṭāī	boriyā	pūzai.
Meaning		ma'nī	ma'nī	ma'na.
Measure	vi. 26	paimāna	paimāna	paimāna.
Measure, to	xi. 51	nāpnā	paimāish k.	kach k.
Meat	i. 34	gosht	gosht	ghwakha.
Medicine		dawā	dārū	dawāī.
Meet, to	viii. 42	milnā	mulāḳī shudan	milyā kedal.
Mend, to	xi. 87	marammat k.	marammat k.	maramat k.
Merchant		saudāgar	tājir	saudāgar.
Mere	ii. 91	ṣirf	ṣirf	ṣirp.
Messenger	vii. 10	ḳāṣid	ḳāṣid	ḳāṣid.
Metalled	ix. 40	pakkā	pukhta	pakha.
Midnight		ādhī rāt	nīmshab	nīmashpa.
Middle		bīch	miyān	myanz.
Milk	iii. 12	dūdh	shīr	paī.
Milk, to	iii. 35	dohnā	doshīdan	lweshal.
Mill, hand-		chakkī	āsyā e dastī	mechan.
Mill, water-		panchakkī	āsyāb	āsyāb.
Mind, to	ii. 20			
Mine, a		khān	kān	kān.
Minute	v. 12	lamḥa	lamḥa	laḥẓa.
Mirror		āīna	āīna	āīna.
Mix, to	iii. 27	milānā	āmekhtan	gaḍ k.
Moist (damp)				
Moment (minute)				
Money		rūpaie	naḳd	naghd.
Monkey		bandar	bozna	bīzo.
Month	ii. 56	mahīnā	māh	miyāsht.
Moon	v. 24	chānd	māh	miyāsht.

English.	*Ref.*	*Urdū.*	*Persian.*	*Pashtū.*
More	xi. 8	aur	ziyāda	zyāt.
Morning	viii. 65	ṣubḥ	ṣubḥ	ṣabā.
Mortar	xi. 8	chūnā	khamīr i āhak	chuna.
Most	ix. 27	akṣar	akṣar	ḍer.
Mother		mā	mādar	mor.
Mould	xii. 11	sāncha	ḳālib	ḳālab.
Mount, to	viii. 3	sawār honā	sawār shudan	swaredal.
Mouse		chūhā	mūsh	muga.
Moustache		mūch	barūt	bret.
Mouth		muṅh	dahān	khluh.
Move, to (act.)		sarkānā	jumbānīdan	khwāzawal.
Much	iv. 20	bahut	bisyār	ḍer.
Mud	ix. 81	kīchaṛ	khilāb	chikaṛe.
Mulberry (tree)	ix. 67	tūt	tūt	tūt.
Mule		khachchar	ḳātir	khachchar.
Musician	xii. 28	bājewālā	muṭrib	dum, bājewāl.
Musket	ix. 27	bandūḳ	tufang	ṭopak.
Mustard		rāī	khardal	sarsham.
Must	ii. 105			
Mutiny		baghāwat	baghāwat	yāghītob.
Mutineer	xii. 20	bāghī	bāghī	yāghī.
Mutton	iii. 31	bherī kā gosht, maṭan	goshti gospand	dapsa ghwakha.
My	i. 1	mer-ā (-e, -ī)	-i-man *or* -am	dzamā.
Nail, iron	xi. 101	preg	mekh	mekh.
Nail, hand		nākhun	nākhun	nūk.
Naked		nangā	birahna	luts lagharṛ.
Name	ii. 21	nām	nām	nūm.
Narrow		saur, tang	tang	tang.
Native country	ii. 53	waṭan	waṭan	waṭan.
Near	ii. 1	nazdīk	nazdīk	nizhde.
Nearly		ḳarīb	ḳarīb	ḳarīb.
Neck		gardan	gardan	gardan.
Necktie		galaband	gulūband	gardan band.
Necessary	iv. 8	ẓarūr	bakār	ẓarūr.
Needle	xi. 101	sūī	sozan	stan.
Negligent	ii. 104	ghāfil	ghāfil	ghāfil.
Never	v. 22	kabhī na	gāhe na	hechere na.
New	ii. 95	naiyā	nau	nauwai.
News	ii. 38	khabar	khabar	khabar.
Newspaper	vii. 18	akhbār	akhbār	akhbar.
Nice		achchhā	khūb	khuh.
Nicely	vii. 7	achchhī ṭaraḥ	ba khūbī	pa khuh shān.
Niche		ṭāḳ	ṭaḳ	ṭāḳ.
Night	ii. 42	rāt	shab	shpa.
Nipple, gun	xii. 10	topī dān	patākhī dān	topī dān.

English.	*Ref.*	*Urdū.*	*Persian.*	*Pashtū.*
Noise	ii. 18	ghul	shor	shor.
None	xi. 16	koī nahīn	hech na	hets na.
Noon	iv. 15	do pahar	nīm roz	gharma.
North		uttar	shimāl	kutub khwā.
Northern	ix. 77	uttar wālā	shimālī	shimālī.
Nose		nāk	bīnī	poza.
Not	i. 66	na, nahīn	na	na.
Note, letter		chiṭṭhī	ruḳ 'a	khaṭṭ.
Nothing		kuch nahīn	hech na	hets na.
Now		abhī, ab	aknūn	os.
Oath		saugand	ḳasam	saugand.
Obey, to		mānnā	farmān bardārī k.	manal.
Obtained, to be	ix. 50	milnā	ḥāṣil shudan	milyā kedal.
O'clock	iii. 34	bajā	nawākht (baja) sā'at	baja.
Officer		sardār	'uhdedār	sardār.
Oil	ii. 90	tel	raughan	tel.
Old	v. 16			
Old, man		buḍhā	pīr	zor, spīngirai.
Old, thing		purānā	kuhna	zor.
Olive	ix. 67	zaitūn	zaitūn	khowan.
On	i. 23	ke upār, par	bālā e, ba	pa—bānde.
Onion		piyāz	piyāz	piyāz.
Only	xi. 39	ṣirf	ṣirf	ṣirp.
Open, to	ii. 8	kholnā	wā k.	lare k.
Or	ii. 48	yā, ki	yā	ka.
Orange	iii. 18	nārangī	nāranj	nāranj.
Order (command)				
Order, to		farmānā	farmūdan	farmāyal.
Other	ii. 110	aur	dīgar	nor.
Our	i. 60	hamārā (-e, -ī)	-i-mā	dzamūng.
Out		bāhar	berūn	bahar.
Over	ix. 5	ūpar	bālā	pās.
Owl		ulū	būm	ulū.
Own	ii. 20	apnā (-e, -ī)	-i-khud	khpul.
Ox		bail	nargāo	ghwāyai.
Pack up, to	viii. 24	band k.	band k.	bandawal.
Pack saddle		pālān	pālān	pālān.
Pace, a	x. 8	ḳadam	ḳadam	ḳadam.
Page	vii. 8	ṣafḥa	ṣafḥa	mukh.
Pain	xiii. 12	dard	dard	dard.
Paint (color)				
Pair		joṛā	juft	joṛā.
Pale		zard	zard	zyar.

English.	*Ref.*	*Urdū.*	*Persian.*	*Pashtū.*
Pan, priming		ranjak dān	ranjak dān	ranjak dān.
Paper	i. 13	kāghaẕ	kaghaẕ	kaghaẕ.
Parapet, of Fort	xii. 29	sīna panāh	sīna panāh	sīna panāh.
Parapet	xi. 75	manderī	dīwār i parda	da tsang dīwāl.
Pare	xi. 98	chhīlnā	tarāshīdan	tsīral.
Parrot		totā	ṭoṭī	ṭoṭī.
Partridge	iii. 38	tītar	durrāj	tsanzarai.
Partridge, striped		chakor	kabk	zarka.
Party	x. 1	madad	madad	madad.
Pass, a	iv. 7	kho	darra	dara.
Pass, to		guẕarnā	guẕashtan	teredal.
Pat, to	viii. 27	tapkī denā	dast mālīdan	lās makhal.
Path, foot	i. 57	pagdandī	rāh i khurd	wara lār.
Patience	ii. 14	ṣabr	ṣabr	ṣabr.
Pattern		namūna	namūna	namūna.
Pay (wages)				
Pea		maṭar	māsh	moth.
Pear	iii. 18	nāshpātī	nāshpātī	naspat.
Peg	ii. 86	khūntī	mekh	mogai.
Pen	vii. 1	ḳalam	ḳalam	ḳalam.
Penal Code, Indian		ta'zīrāt i hind	ta'zīrāt i hind	ta'zīrāt i hind.
Penknife	xi. 97	chāḳū	chāḳū, ḳalam tarāsh	chāḳū.
People		log	khalḳ	khalḳ.
Pepper		mirch	pilpil	mruch.
Perfectly	x. 20	ṭhīk	durust	jukht.
Permanent		pakkā, mustaḳil	mustaḳil	mustaḳil, pokh
Permission		ijāzat	ijāzat	ijāzat.
Perpendicular	xi. 50	sīḍhā	'amūdan	negh.
Persian wheel		arhat	dolāb	arat.
Pestle&mortar		kutak kunḍī	dasta hāwan	molai bagharaī.
Petition		'arẓī	darkhwāst	darkhwāst.
Pickles	iii. 41	achār	achār	achār.
Pick up, to	i. 38	uṭhānā	bardāshtan	porta k.
Pick-axe	xi. 40	gainṭī	kulang	genṭai.
Picture	vii. 14	taṣwīr	taṣwīr	taṣwīr.
Piece	iii. 26	ṭukṛā	pāra	ṭūk.
Pier	xi. 74	pāī	pāī	pkha.
Pierce, to		chhednā	suftan	ārpār yastal.
Pillow	ii. 89	takyā	bālish	bālikht.
Pin	xi. 31	pīn, ālpīn, sūī	sozan, mekh	stan, maugai.
Pine apple		annanās	annanās	annanās.
Pistol	i. 43	pistol, tamānchī	tufangcha	tamāncha.
Pistachio nuts	iii. 18	pista	pista	pista.

English.	*Ref.*	*Urdū.*	*Persian.*	*Pashtū.*
Pitch, to, tent	viii. 18	kharā k.	istāda k.	darawul.
Pitcher		gharā	sabo	garai.
Place	x. 21	jagah	jā	dzāe.
Plainly	xi. 3	ṣāf	saḥīḥ	tsargand.
Plan	vii. 4	naḳsha	naḳsha	naḳsha.
Plane	i. 56	randa	randa	randa.
Plant, to	xi. 53	jamānā	nihāl kardan	būtai lagawal.
Plantain		kelā	mauz	kela.
Plaster	xi. 94	plāstar	astarkārī	plāstar.
Plate		bartan	bushḳāb	tālai.
Play, to	ii. 112	khelnā	bāzī k.	lobe k.
Pleasure		khushī	khurramī	khwakhī.
Plough, a		hal	ḳulba	ḳulba.
Plough, to	ix. 55	hal jotnā	ḳulba rāndan	yawī k.
Pluck, to	iii. 37	par ukhārnā	par kashīdan	par yastal.
Plumb line	xi. 11	sāhul	sahāwul	sahūl.
Pocket		jeb	jeb	jeb.
Poetry	vii. 16	naẓm	naẓm	naẓam.
Pole		ballī	sitūn, tīr	ballai
Pole, tent	viii. 19	chob	chob i khaima	lakara.
Police-station	xi. 83	thānnā	kotwālī	tsaukai.
Polish	i. 65	ṣaiḳal k.	ṣaiḳal k.	ṣaiḳal k.
Polisher		siklī gar	ṣaiḳal gar	ṣaiḳal gar.
Pomegranate	iii. 21	anār	anār	anār.
Pony	viii. 36	ṭaṭṭū	yābū	ṭaṭū.
Poppy		khashkhāsh	khashkhāsh	khashkhāsh.
Poor		gharīb	gharīb	gharīb.
Porter (coolie)				
Post		tham	sitūn	stan.
Post, mail		ḍāk	dāk	ḍāg.
Postage	vii. 11	maḥṣūl	maḥṣūl	maḥṣūl.
Potter	xi. 78	kumhār	kulāl, kūzagar	kulāl.
Potter's wheel		charkh, chāk	charkh i kūzagar	tsarkh.
Pouch	xii. 13	tost dān	tost dān	toshdān.
Pound, for cattle		kānjī haus	maweshī khāna	kānjī ghar.
Pound, to	iii. 28	pīsnā	sāīdan	maida k.
Pour, to	iii. 29	ḍālnā	andākhtan	toyawal.
Prescription		nuskha	nuskha	nuskha.
Present	i. 69	ḥāẓir	ḥāẓir	ḥāẓir.
Preserves	iii. 18	murabbā	murabbā	murabbā.
Prevailing	xiii. 4			
Price	vi. 5	dām	ḳīmat	baya.
Priming		ranjak	ranjak	ranjak.
Principal	vi. 24	aṣl	aṣl	aṣl.
Print, to	vii. 13	chhāpnā	maṭbū' k.	chāp k.
Printer	vii. 18	chhāpne wālā	muṭbi'	chāp kawunkai

English.	*Ref.*	*Urdū.*	*Persian.*	*Pashtū.*
Prison		je khāna	ḳaid khāna	ḳaid khāna.
Prisoner		ḳaidī	ḳaidī	ḳaidī, bandī.
Procrastination.		tāl māholī	lait o la'l	zanḍ.
Promise	ii. 65	wa 'da	wa'da	wāda.
Promotion		taraḳḳī	taraḳḳī	taraḳḳī.
Pronounce	vii. 5	talaffuẓ k.	talaffuẓ k.	talaffuẓ k.
Properly		achchhī ṭaraḥ se	ba khūbī	pa khuh shān sara.
Prose	vii. 16	naṣr	naṣr	naṣar.
Proverb	vii. 15	maṣal	maṣal	matal.
Pull (drag)				
Pulse	xiii. 21	nabẓ	nabẓ	nabẓ.
Punkha	ii. 71	pankhā	bād kash	pakai.
Punish, to	ii. 110	sazā denā	sazā dādan	saza warkawal.
Punishment		sazā	sazā	saza.
Pure, metal	vi. 21	khāliṣ	khaliṣ	kara.
Purgative	xiii. 16	jalāb	mushil	jāṛ.
Put out, to	ii. 10	bujhānā	gul k.	mṛah k.
Quail		baterā	būdna	maraza
Quarter	v. 7	pāo *or* chauthāī	chahārum ḥiṣṣa, ruba'	tsalorana.
Question		suwāl	suwāl	suwāl.
Quit (leave go)				
Quick		jald	zūd	zar.
Quickly	ii. 15	jaldī	ba zūdī	zar.
Quiet (silent)				
Quiet, tame	viii. 43	gharīb	gharīb	asīl.
Quince	iii. 18	bihī	bihī	bihai.
Quite	iv. 10	khūb	bi-l-kull	tuk.
Radiating	xi. 13	chalākī meṅ	māil ba markaz	markaz ta māil.
Rafter		kaṛī	tīr	tīr.
Rag	xiii. 25	kapṛā	lattā	tsīṛra.
Rain, to	i. 57	pānī paṛna	bārān shudan	bārān kedal.
Rainbow		dhanuk	ḳaus i ḳuzaḥ	da budaī tāl.
Raise, to		unchā k.	buland k.	porta k.
Raised, to be, a regiment	xii. 1	khaṛā honā	muḳarrar sh.	muḳarrarkedal
Raisin	iii. 16	kishmish	munaḳḳā	mawīz.
Ram, to	xi. 95	kūṭnā	kuftan	ṭakawal.
Ramrod		gaz	gaz	gaz.
Rammer	xi. 42	dūrmaṭ	gil kob	durmaṭ.
Rank	xii. 4	'uhda	'uhda	'uhda.
Rat (mouse)				
Ravine	ix. 18	nālā	āb rau, jū	khwaṛ.
Razor		ustara	pākī, ustara	pākaī.

English.	*Ref.*	*Urdū.*	*Persian.*	*Pashtū.*
Read, to	vii. 2	paṛhnā	khwāndan	lwustal.
Ready	ii. 75	taiyār	taiyār	joṛ.
Reason	ii. 107	sabab	sabab	sabab.
Rebate	xi. 81	patām	jarī	patām.
Rebellion		balwā	baghāwat	yāghīgarī.
Receive	xi. 2	pānā	yāftan	mundal.
Receipt		rasīd	ḳabz ul waṣūl	rasīd.
Recipe (prescription)				
Recognize	ii. 31	pahchānnā	shinākhtan	pezhandal.
Red	iii. 30	lāl	surkh	sūr.
Reed	viii. 73	sarkandā	nai	darwai.
Reins		rās	ligām	bāge.
Regiment	xii. 1	palṭan	dasta-i-sipāh	palṭan.
Relate, to		bayān k.	bayān k.	bayān k.
Relation, a		rishtadār	rishtadār	rishtadār.
Relationship		rishtadārī	rishtadarī	khpalwī.
Remain, to	v. 1	rahnā	māndan	osedal.
Remember, to	ii. 4	yād rakhnā	yād dāshtan	yād laral.
Renew, to	xi. 84			
Rest		ārām	ārām	ārām.
Rest, to	viii. 46	muḳām k.	ḳaiyām k.	ṭikāo k.
Reservoir		tālāb	hauz	tālāb.
Return, to	ii. 30	phir ānā	bāz āmadan	rāgarzedal.
Reward		in'ām	in'ām	in'ām.
Rheumatism	xiii. 3	bāī	rīh	bād.
Rhinoceros		kargadan	kargadan, k.	genḍaī.
Rib		paslī	ustukhwān i pahlū	pukhtaī.
Rich		daulatmand	ghanī	dunyadār.
Rice	vi. 15	chāṅwal	birinj	wrīzhe.
Riding	ix. 2	sawār	sawār	swoṛ.
Rifle	xii. 7	rafal	tufang i rakhdār	rakhdār ṭupak jazāil.
Right, hand	ii. 12	dāhinā	rāst	shai lās.
Right (correct)				
Right angles, at	x. 17	gunyā meṅ	'amūd	khī guṭ.
Rind	iii 22.	chhilkā	post	postakai.
Ring		chhalā	ḥalḳa	ḥalḳa.
Ring, finger		angūṭhī	angushtarī	guta.
Ring, to	xi. 64			
Ripe	iii. 30	pakkā	pukhta	pakh.
Rise, to, sun, &c.	v. 24	nikalnā	ṭulū 'shudan	rākhatal.
Rise, to make birds	viii. 74			
River	viii. 2	naddī	daryā	sīnd.

English.	*Ref.*	*Urdū.*	*Persian.*	*Pashtū.*
Road	viii. 5	rastā	rāh	lār
Roast, to	iii. 17	kabāb k.	kabāb k.	kabāb k.
Robbery		chorī	duzdī	ghlā
Rod	x. 13	gaz	gaz	hamsa
Roof	xi. 12	chhat	saḳf	koṭah
Room		kamara	ḥujra	ḥujra
Room, space	xi. 34	jagah	jāe	dzāe
Root	i. 53	jaṛ	bekh	wulī
Rope	i. 38	rassī	respān	purai
Rose		gulāb	gul i surkh	gulāb
Rosewater		gulāb kā 'araḳ	gulāb	da gulābo 'araḳ
Rot, to	i. 66	murjhānā	pazhmurda sh.	mur kedal
Round		gol	mudawwar	gaṛd
Round, to go	viii. 42	ghumnā	gardīdan	gardedal
Rub, to	viii. 63	malnā	mālīdan	mukhal
Ruby		la'l	la'l, yāḳūt	yāḳūt
Rudder		paswār	paswār, H.	singāwaṅṛ
Rug		ḳālīcha	ḳālīn	kālīn
Ruler	xi. 96	misṭar	misṭar	misṭar
Run, to	i. 70	dauṛnā	dawīdan	zghaledal
Run, to (flow)				
Rusty	xii. 8	morchā khāyā hūā	zangdār	zangdār.
Saddle	iv. 15	zīn	zīn	zīn
Safe		salāmtī se	bā amān	salāmat
Safety		salāmtī	amān	salāmatya
Sailor		mānjī	mallāḥ	maiṅṛgai
Salt	iii. 41	namak	namak	mālga
Same	v. 19	ekhī, yahī	hamīn, hamān	ham dagha
Sand	xi. 39	ret	reg	shuge
Sand grouse	viii. 70	bantītar	baghal ḳara	tsanzarai, sīsaī
Sapphire		nīlam	ṣafīr	ṣafīr
Saucer	iii. 9	pirich	na'lbakī	rekābaī
Saucepan		degchī	degcha, deg	degchai
Saw	xi. 18	ārā	arra	ara
Say, to	ii. 49	kahnā	guftan	wayal
Scabbard	xii. 12	miyān	miyān	tuka
Scaffold	xi. 88	ṣandalī	ṣandalī	andarpāya
Scales	vi. 20	tarāzū	tarāzū	tulah
School	vii. 17	madrasa	madrasa	madrasa.
Scimitar	i. 65	talwār	shamsher	tūra.
Scissors	xi. 102	ḳainchī	miḳrāẓ	byātaī.
Scorpion	ix. 72	bichchhū	kazhdum	laṛam.
Scoundrel	ii. 100	badma'āsh	badma'āsh	badkār.
Scrape, to (pare)				
Scratch, to	i. 52	chhīlnā	kharāshīdan	ghutsawal.

English.	*Ref.*	*Urdū.*	*Persian.*	*Pashtū.*
Scratch out, to		miṭānā	maḥw k.	maḥwa k.
Screw	xi. 23	pech	pech	pech.
Screwdriver		pech kash	pech kash	pech kash.
Screen, sieve	xi. 68	chhānnā	g̲h̲irbāl	parwẹzai.
Screen, curtain		parda	parda	parda.
Sea		samūndar	baḥr	kārī daryāb.
Seal	vii. 11	muhr	muhr	muhr.
Search, to	ii. 43	talāsh k.	justan	laṭawal.
Season		mausim	mausam	mosam.
Second	vii. 8	dūsrā	doyum	dwayam.
Sedan	ix. 3	dolī	pālkī	pālkai.
See, to	i. 35	dekhnā	dīdan	katal.
Seed		bīj	tuk̲h̲m	tuk̲h̲m.
Seer	vi. 11	sīr	aṣār	ser.
Seize	vi. 22	pakaṛnā	giriftan	nīwal.
Sell, to	vi. 29	bechnā	farok̲h̲tan	k̲h̲artsawal.
Send, to	i. 30	bhejnā	faristādan	legal.
Sentry	xii. 6	pahrewālā	pāsbān	pahra dār.
Servant	i. 31	naukar	mulāzim	naukar.
Serve, to	xii. 3	naukrī k.	mulāzimat k.	naukarī k.
Severe	ii. 110	sak̲h̲t	sak̲h̲t	sak̲h̲t.
Sew, to	i. 70	sīnā	dok̲h̲tan	gaṇḍal.
Shade	ii. 73	fānūs	fānūs	panūs.
Shake, to	i. 55, & x. 22	hilānā	jumbānīdan	tsanḍawal.
Shame		sharm	sharm	sharm.
Shape	ii. 98	shakl	shakl	shekl.
Sherbet	iii. 15	sharbat	sharbat	sharbat.
Shawl	vi. 10	shāl	shāl	shāla.
She	i. 29	wuh, yih	o	dā, hag̲h̲a.
Sheep	i. 32	bheṛ	gospand, mesh	gud.
Sheepskin	ii. 103	postīn	postīn	postīn.
Sheeshum	ix. 67	shīsham, sīsū		shawā.
Sheet		chaddar	chaddar	tsādar.
Shelf	ii. 74	tak̲h̲ta	tak̲h̲ta	ṭāḳ.
Shine, to	i. 65	chamaknā	darak̲h̲shīdan	dzaledal.
Shivering	xiii. 19	larza	larza	larza.
Ship		nāo	jahāz	jahāz.
Shirt		kamīs	pairāhan, kamīs	kuṛtā.
Shoe	ii. 74	jūtī	pāe posh	panṛe.
Shoemaker		mochī	paizār doz, *or* kafsh doz	mochī.
Shoot, to		bandūḳ chalānā	bandūḳ sar k. *or* chalānīdan H.	topak chalawal
Shoot, to, game		shikār khelnā	ṣaid k.	kk̲h̲kār k.
Shooting *or* hunting		shikār	shikār	kk̲h̲kār.

English.	*Ref.*	*Urdū.*	*Persian.*	*Pashtū.*
Shop	ii. 92	dukān	dukān	dukān, aṭāī.
Short	i. 12	chhoṭā	khurd	wor.
Shot, small		chharrā	ṣāchma	chare.
Shot, gun	xii. 16	golā	gola	golaī.
Shoulder	xiii. 24	kāndhā	shāna, dosh	muṭ.
Show, to		dikhlānā	namūdan, nishān dādan	khāyal.
Shrink	xi. 57	ghaṭnā	kotāh gashtan	waṛūkai k. *or* landedal.
Shut	ii. 70	band	band	pūra.
Shut, to	ii. 8	band k.	band k.	pūra k..
Sick, ill		bīmār	marīẓ	randzūr nājoṛ.
Sickness (vomit)				
Side	viii. 42	ṭaraf	ṭaraf	khwā.
Siege		muḥāṣara, ḳil'a bandī	muḥāṣara	ḳil'a bandī.
Sieve (screen)				
Sift, to	xi. 68	chhānnā	bekhtan	chaṅṛawul.
Sight, a		tamāsha	tamāsha	tamāsha.
Sight	ix. 9	naẓr	naẓr	naẓar.
Silent	ii. 3	chup	khāmosh	chup.
Silver	vi. 20	chāndī	sīm	spin zar.
Sing, to		gānā	sarāīdan	sandare wāyal.
Sink, to	ix. 81	phasjānā, dūbnā	faro raftan	dūbedal.
Sir	ii. 57	ṣāḥib, jī	ṣāḥib, janāb	ṣāḥiba.
Sister	i. 5	bahin	khwāhar, hamshīra	khor.
Sit, to	ii. 24	baiṭhnā	nishistan	kenāstal.
Skin		chamṛā	charm	tsarman.
Skin, to	iii. 37	khāl utārnā	post kashīdan	postakai yastal
Sky	iv. 10	āsmān	āsmān	āsmān.
Skylight		khirkī	tābdān	roshandān.
Slake, to	xi. 92	bhaṛkānā	khamīr k.	khamīr k.
Slave	vi. 23	ghulām	ghulām	ghulām.
Sleep		nīnd	khwāb	khob.
Sleep, to	iv, 16	sonā	khuspīdan	khob k.
Sleeve		āstīn	astīn	lastāṅṛai.
Slip, to	i. 60	phisalnā	laghzīdan	khoedal.
Slippery	i. 57	phislī	laghzān	khuyana.
Slight	xii. 25	khafīf	khafīf	lug.
Slope	ix. 42	salāmī	salāmī	salāmī.
Sloping	ix. 42	salāmī meṅ	salāmī dār	salāmī.
Slow, a horse, &c.	i. 9	sust	sust, kam rāh	sust.
Slowly	ix. 31	āhisti	āhisti	roro.
Small	iii. 26	chhoṭā	khurd	woṛ.

English.	*Ref.*	*Urdū.*	*Persian.*	*Pashtū.*
Smell, to	i. 46	sūnghnā	boīdan	boe k.
Smoke		dhūāṅ	dūd	lūgai.
Smooth	i. 56	chiknā	hamwār	hamwār.
Snake	ix. 72	sāmp	mār	mār.
Snipe	viii. 67	chāhā	karak	kakuwai
Snow	iv. 4	barf	barf	barf.
Snuff		naswār	naswār	naswār.
Soap		sābūn	sābūn	sabūn.
So	ii. 36	aisā	īn ṭaur	dāse.
Soft	viii. 59	narm	narm	narm.
Soil	xi. 37	miṭṭī	gil	khāwra.
Soldier	ix. 6	sipāhī	sipāhī	spāī.
Some	iii. 12	kuchh	ḳadare	tsuh lug.
Son	i. 2	beṭā	pisar	zoe.
Song		gīt	sarod	sandare.
Soon		jaldī	ba zūdī	zar.
Sore, a	xiii. 18	zakhm	zakhm	zakhm.
Sort, kind		ḳism	ḳism	ḳism.
Soup	iii. 5	sharūr	shorba	shorwa.
Sour	iii. 21	khaṭṭā	tursh	trīw.
South		dakkhan	janūb	janūb.
Southern	ix. 77	dakkhan wālā	janūbī	janūbī.
Sow, to	ix. 53	bonā	kāshtan	karal.
Spade	xi. 28	belcha	belcha	yūm.
Span		giṭ	badist	lwesht.
Spark		chingāra	sharāra	batsarai.
Speak, to	ii. 49	bolnā	guftan	wayal.
Spectacles		chashmak	'ainak	chashme.
Speech		taḳrīr	taḳrīr	taḳrīr.
Speech, oration		khuṭba	khuṭba	khuṭba.
Spice	iii. 28	maṣālaḥ	maṣālaḥ	maṣālaḥ
Spider		makṛī	'ankabūt	julāgai.
Spin, to		kātnā	tanīdan	oudal.
Spinning wheel		charkhā	charkha	tsarkha.
Spit	iii. 38	sīkh	sīkh	sīkh
Spit, to		thūknā	tuf k.	tūkal.
Splash, to	xi. 90	chiṛknā	andākhtan	chaṛkāo k.
Spleen		tilī	ṭiḥāl	ṭiḥāl.
Split, to	i. 53	chīrnā	shigāftan, shāk [k.	tsīral.
Split, a		chīr	chāk	chāk.
Sponge		isfanj	isfanj	isfanj.
Spoon	iii. 15	chamcha	chamcha	tsamtsa.
Sprain	xiii. 23	moch	pech	khatalai.
Spread, to	viii. 40	bichhānā	gustarānīdan	ghoṛawal.
Spring	iv. 5	chashma	chashma	chīna.
Spring, the	iv. 17	bahār	bahār	bahār, sparlai.
Sprinkle, to	ii. 83	chiṛknā	pāshīdan	chiṛkāo k.

English.	*Ref.*	*Urdū.*	*Persian.*	*Pashtū.*
Sprout, to	ix. 53	ugnā	bar āmadan	zargh ūnedal.
Square, a	xi. 11	gunyā	ķāima, gunya	ķāima.
Square		chaukonā	murabba' [H.	tsalor guṭai.
Stable		isṭabal	asṭabal	asṭabal.
Stack	xi. 7	chattā	toda	ḍerai.
Stack, to		karwanja lagā-nā, dherī la-gānā	toda k.	ḍerai k.
Staff, levelling	x. 10	gaz	neza	janḍa.
Staircase		sīrhī	zīna, nardbān	andarpaya.
Stale	iii. 24	bāsī	bisyār roza	begānai.
Stand, to	ii. 23	khaṛā honā	istāda shudan	daredal
Stand still, to (remain)				
Star		tārā	sitāra	storai.
Start, to	viii. 45	rawāna honā	rawāna shudan	rawānedal.
Stay, to		thahrnā	māndan	osedal.
Steal, to	i. 40	churānā	ba duzdī bur-dan	ghlā k.
Steam		dhūāṅ	dukhān, dūd	lūgai.
Steel		ispād, faulād	fāulad	faulād.
Step (pace)				
Steep	ix. 42	khaṛā	istāda	negh.
Steining	ix. 57			
Stick	i. 27	lāṭhī	chob i dastī	largai.
Stiff, clay	xi. 38	chiknā	charb	zīga.
Stir, to	iii. 15	hilānā	jumbānīdan	khwazawal.
Stirrup	viii. 6	rikāb	rikāb	rikāb.
Stomach	xiii. 11	pet	shikam	geḍa.
Stone	i. 21	patthar	sang	kāṅṛai.
Stone (in bladder)		patthrī	sang i maṣāna	sang i maṣāna.
Stony	ix. 24	patthrelā	sanglakhī	kaṅṛīza.
Stop, to (act.)	ii. 42	roknā	istāda k.	daṛawal.
Store		godām	asbāb khāna	asbāb khāna.
Storm	iv. 24	āndhī	ṭūfān	silai.
Studded		jarā hūā	muraṣṣa'	muraṣṣa'.
Straight	ii. 81	sīdhā	rāst	negh.
Straw, a		tinkā	kāh	khalai.
Straw, bedding	viii. 40	bichhālī	kāh	lūkha.
Strike, to (gong)	v. 25	bajānā	zadan	ghagawal.
String	xi. 14	sūt	tār	mazai.
Strong	xi. 88	maẓbūṭ	maẓbūṭ	maẓbūṭ.
Stumble, to		ṭhokar khānā	budrī khwur-dan, sikanda-rī khwurdan	budrī khwaṛal.
Subscription		chandā	chandā	chanda.

English.	*Ref.*	*Urdū.*	*Persian.*	*Pashtū.*
Subtract, to	v. 1	minhāī k.	minhā k.	tafrīķ k.
Sugar	iii. 11	miṣrī	ķand	nabāt.
Suit, clothes	ii. 95	joṛā	jora (H.)	joṛa.
Summer	iv. 9	garmī	mausim i garm	oṛai.
Sun		sūraj	āftāb	nmar.
Sunrise	viii. 45	sūraj nikalnā	tulū' i āftāb	da nmar khatal
Superstructure	xi. 5	'imārat ūpar kī	kār i bālā	da pās kār.
Supplies	ix. 50	rasad	ajnās	rasad.
Supply, to		pahunchānā	rasānīdan	rasawal.
Swallow, a		ab bīl	abābīl	abābīl.
Swallow, to	iii. 22	nigalnā	faro burdan	nagharal.
Swamp(marsh)				
Sweep, to	ii. 113	jhāṛnā	ruftan	jārū k.
Sweeper		mihtar	khāk rob	metar.
Sweet	iii. 21	mīthā	shīrīn	khog.
Sweetmeat	iii. 24	mithāī	shīrīnī	khwāguh.
Swift	i. 9	tez rau	tez rau	gaṛandai.
Swim, to	ix. 80	pairnā	shināwarī k.	lanbowahal.
Switch	ix. 68	ķamchī	ķamchīn	lakhta.
Sword		kirich	shamsher, ṣaif	tūra.
Symptom	xiii. 9	nishānī	'alāmat	nakha.
Table	i. 20	mez	mez	mez.
Tailor		darzī	khaiyāṭ	darzī.
Take, to	i. 43	lenā	giriftan	ākhustal.
Take away, to	iii. 18	lejānā	burdan	wṛal.
Talk, to	i. 73	guftgū k.	guftgū k.	khabare k.
Tall	i. 11	lanbā	buland	lwaṛ.
Tank (reservoir)				
Tape	x. 7	fītā	fīta	mazai.
Target		chānd, nishān	nishān, āmāj	nakha.
Tea	iii. 4	chā	chāe	chāe.
Teapot		chā pōchī	chāedān	chādān.
Telescope		durbīn	durbīn	durbīn.
Tell, to	ix. 37	kahnā	guftan	wayal.
Temple	viii. 13	mandir	but ķada	darmsāl.
Temporary		kachā, chand roza	chand roza	chand roza.
Tent	viii. 16	ḍerā	khaima	khema.
That	i. 2	wuh	ān	hagha.
Than	i. 11	se	az	la ... na.
Their	i. 3	unkā (-ke -kī)	-i-eshān	da hagho.
Then	ii. 12	tab	ān waķt, bāz	no, hagha wakht.
There	ii. 23	wahāṅ, udhar	ān jā, ān sū	halta.
They	i. 24	we, ye	eshān	haghoī.
Thick	i. 13	moṭā	luk, purkār, ghalī	ghaṭ.
Thief	ii. 110	chor	duzd	ghal.

English.	*Ref.*	*Urdū.*	*Persian.*	*Pashtū.*
Thin		patlā	bārīk	māhīn.
Thin (lean)				
Thing		chīz	chīz	tsīz.
Think, to	iv. 14	samajhnā	pindāshtan	khiyal k.
Third, a	v. 6	tihāī	ṣulṣ, soyumī ḥiṣṣa	dreyama ḥiṣa.
This	i. 1.	yih	īn	dā.
Thorn	ix. 69	kāṇṭā	khār	aghzai.
Thread		sūt	tār, rishta	mazai.
Thread, screw	xi. 23	chūṛī	shigāf	manz.
Threat		dhamkī	takhwīf	daṛaka.
Threaten		dhamkānā	tarsānīdan	wyarawul.
Throat		gala	ḥalḳ	ḥalḳ.
Through	viii. 31	meṅ se	az miyān-i-	la na.
Throughout	xi. 65	andar bāhar se	derūn o berūn	bekhī.
Throw, to	i. 37	pheṅknā	andākhtan	ghurzawul.
Throw away		pheṅk deṇā	andākhtan	ghurzawul.
Thumb		angūṭhā	angusht i nar	ghaṭa guta.
Thunder	iv. 20	garj	ra'd	brekhna.
Tie, to	ii. 93	bāṇḍhnā	bastan	taṛul.
Tiger		sher, bāgh	palang	zmarai.
Tight		tang	tang, chust	tang, chust.
Tighten, to, girth	viii. 32			
Tile	xi. 79	khaprā, nariyā	sifāl	kapra.
Till	iii. 36	tak	tā	pa pore.
Time	v. 9	waḳt, bajā	waḳt	wakht.
Time, in		waḳt par	bar waḳt	pa wakht.
Tin		ḳala'ī	ḳala'ī	kalaī.
Tired	i. 72	thakā	mānda	stuṛai.
Title		laḳab	laḳab	khiṭāb.
To	i. 18	ko	rā, ba	ta.
To-day	ii. 46	āj	imroz	nun.
Toe		pāṅw kī unglī	angusht i pā	da pkhe guta.
Together		sang	bāham	sara.
To-morrow	i. 57	kal	fardā	ṣabā.
To-night	xii. 5	āj rāt	imshab	nun shpa.
Tongs		chimṭā	ātashgīr	nūsai.
Tongue	xiii. 22	jīb	zabān	zhaba.
Tool	xi. 70	auzār	auzār	asbāb.
Tooth		dānt	dandān	ghākh.
Tooth-brush	ii. 94	miswāk	miswāk	miswāk.
Tooth-pick		dand, khilāl	khilāl	khilāl.
Tooth-powder	ii. 94	manjan	misī	manjan.
Top, hill-	viii. 1	chotī	ḳulla	tsuka.
Torch		mash'al	mash'al	mashāl.
Touch, to	x. 13	lagnā, chūnā	chaspīdan, mas k., dast zadan	lagedal, mas k.

English.	*Ref.*	*Urdū.*	*Persian.*	*Pashtū.*
Tower	xii. 15	burj	burj	burz.
Town	v. 13	ḳaṣba	ḳariya	kalai.
Toy	ii. 112	khilonā	bāzīcha	guḍaī.
Traitor	xii. 21	namak ḥarām	namak ḥarām	namak ḥarām.
Translation	ix. 36	tarjuma	tarjuma	tarjuma.
Travel, to		safar k.	siyāḥat k.	safar k.
Traveller		musāfir	saiyāḥ	musāfir.
Tribe	ix. 28	ḳaum	ḳabīla	ḳaum, khel.
Trick	ii. 91	fareb	fareb	fareb.
Trotting	viii. 30	dulkī	ba poya	dulkī.
Trousers		panṭlūn	pāe jāma	paṛtūg.
Trowel	xi. 10	karnī	gil māla	karanḍaī.
True	ii. 40	sach	rāst	rikhtiyā.
Trumpet	xii. 28	ḳarnā	ḳarnā	surnā.
Trunk, elephant's		sūnḍ	khaṛṭūm	khaṛtam.
Truss	xi. 17	ḳainchī	ḳainchī	kainchaī.
Turban	ii. 79	pagṛī	dastār	pagṛaī.
Turmeric		haldī	zard chob	kurkaman.
Turn, to	ii. 12	phirnā	gashtan	garzedal.
Turnip		shalgham	shalgham	ṭipar, shalgham
Twice	v. 13	do chand	do chand	dwa chand.
Twist, to (neut)	xi. 21	teṛha honā	pechīda shudan	kagedal.
Ugly	i. 10	badṣūrat	bad shakl	bad rang.
Umbrella		chhātā	chatr	tsatraī.
Uncle, *p.*	i. 7	chachā	'ammū	truh
Uncle, *m.*		māmāṅ	māmūn	māmā.
Under	i. 24	ke nīche	zer-i-	da—lānde.
Underburnt	xi. 63	kam pakkā	kam pukhta	nīm pokh.
Understand, to	ix. 34	samajhnā	fahmīdan	pohedal.
Unless	xi. 4			
Unmetalled	ix. 40	kachchā	khām	kacha.
Unwilling		kām chor	rāghib na	rāghib na.
Up		ūpar	bālā	pās.
Upright	viii. 19	sīḍhā	rāst	negh.
Upper	xi. 62	ūpar kā	-i-bālā	da pās.
Use, to		kām meṅ lānā	ba kār awurdan isti'māl k.	pa kār rāwṛal.
Useful		kām kā	mufīd	fāidamand.
Vacant (empty)				
Valley	x. 18	maidān	maidān, wādī darra	darra.
Vegetable	iii. 27	tarkārī	sabzī	ṣābuh.
Very	ii. 85	bahut	bisyār	ḍer.

English.	*Ref.*	*Urdū.*	*Persian.*	*Pashtū.*
Vicious	viii. 43	badma'āsh	badma'āsh	kam aṣl.
Victory	xii. 27	jīt	fatḥ	barai.
Village	v. 19	gāṅw	dih	kalai.
Villager	iii. 35	gāṅwālā	dihḳān	kalīwāl.
Vinegar		sirkā	sirka	sirka.
Violet, flower		binafsha	binafsha	nā farmān.
Volume	vii. 8	jild	jild	jild.
Vomiting	xiii. 10	ḳai	istifrāgh	ḳai.
Wages	ii. 51	ṭalab	tankhwāh	mawājib.
Waist		kamar	kamar	mlā.
Wait, to	v. 12	thahrnā	māndan	daredal.
Wake, to	ii. 33	jagānā	bedār k.	wīkhawal.
Walk, to	ix. 21	ḳadam ḳadam ch.	ḳadam ḳadam r.	ḳadam ḳadam tlul.
Walk about, to	i. 72	phirnā	sair kardan	garzedal.
Wall	xi. 15	dīwāl	dīwār	dīwāl.
Wall-plate		dāsā	kateba	dāsā.
Walnut		akhroṭ	chār maghaz	akhroṭ.
Want, to (wish)				
War		laṛāī	jang	jang.
Warm	ii. 79	garm	garm	garm.
Warning	ii. 110	'ibrat	'ibrat	'ibrat.
Wash, to	i. 51	dhonā	shustan	wīndzal.
Washerman	ii. 61	dhobī	gāzar	dobī.
Wasp		bhar	zanbūr	banbara.
Watchman	viii. 24	chokīdār	pāsbān	tsokīdār.
Water	i. 33	pānī	āb	obuh.
Water-bag		masak	mashk	mashk.
Water-carrier		bishtī	saḳā	mashkī.
Water-course		nālā	jū, rūd khāna	lakhtai.
Water-fowl		murghābī	murghābī	elāī.
Wax		mom	mom	mom.
Way (road)				
Weak	xii. 17	kam zor	kam zor	kam zor.
Weave, to		bunnā	bāftan	
Weaver		julāhā	bāfanda	
We	i. 32	ham	mā	mūng.
Week	v. 11	hafta	hafta	hafta.
Weigh, to	vi. 20	tolnā	sanjīdan	talal.
Well	viii. 63	achchhī ṭaraḥ	ba khūbī	pa khuh shān.
Well, a	ix. 57	kūāṅ	chāh	koyai.
West		pachchham	maghrib	maghrib.
Wet, to	xiii. 25	bhigonā	tar k.	lamdawal.
What?		kyā?	chi?	tsuh?
What sort?	i. 22	kaisā?	chi ṭaur?	tsuh ranga.
Wheat	ix. 51	gehūṅ	gandum	ghanam.

English.	*Ref.*	*Urdū.*	*Persian.*	*Pashtū.*
Wheel	xi. 41	paihyā	charkh, i'rāba	pāya.
Wheelbarrow	xi. 41	hāth gāṛhī	gardūn	lās gāḍī.
When?		kab	kai	kulah.
When	ii. 63	jab	chūn, waḳte ki	kūm wakht chi.
Whence?		kahāṅ se?	az kujā?	la charta na.
Where		jahāṅ	jāe ki	kūm zāi chi.
Where?	i. 25	kahāṅ?	kujā?	charta, kūm zāi?
Which		jo	ki	chi.
Which?		kaunsā?	kudām?	kūm?
Whip	ii. 96	koṛā, chābuk	ḳamchīn	chābuk.
White	viii. 61	sufed	sufed	spīn.
Who		jo	ki	chi.
Who?	i. 15	kaun?	ki? kudām?	kūm?
Whom?		kaun? kis ko?	kirā?	kūm?
Why	ii. 36	kyūn, kis wāsṭe	chirā	wale *or* tsulā.
Wick		battī	fatīla	patīla, battaī.
Wide		chauṛā	pahanāwar	plan.
Wife	i. 8	jorū	zoja, ḳabīla	ṭabar.
Willing		miḥnatī	tandih	miḥnatī.
Willow	ix. 67	bed majnū	bed	wula.
Wind		hawā	bād	bād.
Window	ii. 76	khirkī	darīcha	kaṛkaī.
Wine	i. 58	sharāb	sharāb	sharāb.
Winter (cold weather)				
Wise		'aḳlmand	'āḳil	hokhyār.
Wish, to	viii. 60	chāhnā	khwāstan	ghukhtal.
With	ii. 108	sāṭh	hamrāh	sara.
Within		andarūn	andarūn	da nuna.
Without	ii. 107	be	be, baghair	be.
Wolf		bheṛiyā	gurg	lewuh.
Woman	i. 5	'aurat	zan	khaza.
Wonderful		'ajīb	'ajab	'ajab.
Wood	iii. 39	lakṛī	chob	largai.
Wool		ūn	pashm	waṛaī.
Word	vii. 12	lafẓ	lafẓ	lafẓ.
Work		kām	kār	kār.
Workman	ix. 7	mazdūr	mazdūr	muzdūr.
World		jahān	dunyā	dunyā.
Wound		zakhm	zakhm	zakhm.
Wounded	xii. 24	zakhmī	zakhmi	zakhmī.
Write, to	vii. 1	likhnā	nawishtan	līkal.
Wrong	ii. 98	nā durust	nā durust	khuh na.
Year	v. 18	baras	sāl	kāl.
Yesterday	iv. 11	kal	dīroz	parūn.
Yet	ii. 62	abtak	hinoz, ilḥāl	os.

English.	*Ref.*	*Urdū.*	*Persian.*	*Pashtū.*
Yellow	xi. 63	pīlā	zard	zyaṛ.
You	i. 33	tum	shumā	tāso.
Young		jawān	jawān	dzawān.
Young one		bachcha	bachcha	bachai.
Your	i. 2	tumhārā (-e, -i)	-i-shumā	stā.
Youth, a		jawān	jawān	dzwān.